IMAGES OF WAR

KNIGHT'S CROSS WINNERS OF THE WAFFEN SS

RARE PHOTOGRAPHS FROM WARTIME ARCHIVES

IMAGES OF WAR

KNIGHT'S CROSS WINNERS OF THE WAFFEN SS

RARE PHOTOGRAPHS FROM WARTIME ARCHIVES

MARC RIKMENSPOEL

Pen & Sword
MILITARY

First published in Great Britain in 2020 by
PEN & SWORD MILITARY
An imprint of
Pen & Sword Books Ltd
Yorkshire – Philadelphia

ISBN 978 1 52676 758 5

A CIP catalogue record for this book is
available from the British Library.

Typeset by Mac Style
Printed and bound in the UK by CPI Group (UK) Ltd, Croydon, CRO 4YY

FSC www.fsc.org MIX Paper from responsible sources FSC® C013604

Pen & Sword Books Limited incorporates the imprints of Atlas, Archaeology, Aviation, Discovery, Family History, Fiction, History, Maritime, Military, Military Classics, Politics, Select, Transport, True Crime, Air World, Frontline Publishing, Leo Cooper, Remember When, Seaforth Publishing, The Praetorian Press, Wharncliffe Local History, Wharncliffe Transport, Wharncliffe True Crime and White Owl.

For a complete list of Pen & Sword titles please contact

PEN & SWORD BOOKS LIMITED
47 Church Street, Barnsley, South Yorkshire, S70 2AS, England
E-mail: enquiries@pen-and-sword.co.uk
Website: www.pen-and-sword.co.uk

Or

PEN AND SWORD BOOKS
1950 Lawrence Rd, Havertown, PA 19083, USA
E-mail: Uspen-and-sword@casematepublishers.com
Website: www.penandswordbooks.com

Introduction

The Waffen-SS was many things. It was an elite force of carefully-recruited men with superior physiques. It was an assembly of foreigners, some with no affiliation with Germany or far-right politics. It was armored divisions, mountain divisions, infantry formations, and even horsed cavalry. The Waffen-SS defies generalization.

The men portrayed in this book were volunteers, unlike many soldiers conscripted or assigned to the Waffen-SS later in the war. Most wanted to be soldiers, while others were reservists who originally served as uniformed policemen or political activists. The SS existed to advance Nazi ideology, though over time it came to represent itself, for example in carrying out a foreign policy distinct from that of Nazi Germany's Foreign Ministry. The men who served in the military branch of the SS, the Waffen-SS, from before the war, or from the early phase of the war, understood that part of their role was to be more than soldiers, by advancing SS and Nazi policies.

This was shown by the participation of Waffen-SS elements in the activities of the Einsatzgruppen murder squads, and in other killings of prisoners and civilians. The invasions of Poland and the Soviet Union were intended to lead to the enslavement of those countries, and German casual cruelty was displayed by many parts of the occupation forces, not only the SS and its military Waffen-SS. This also happened to a lesser extent in other occupied territories.

With all this said, the Waffen-SS primarily fought as soldiers, and often at the most important points of the Western and Eastern Fronts. The fighting in the Soviet Union was some of the largest-scale, long-lasting, and most-intense in all of history. The Waffen-SS expanded in an attempt to meet the needs of a prolonged war, and most of its senior units became armored or partially-armored.

The Waffen-SS possessed press and propaganda services proportionally far greater than those of the rest of the German military. The early Waffen-SS divisions fought in many significant battles, and received extensive coverage of their participation. This extended to a liberal distribution of medals and awards, and many photographs of the decorated men.

Some of those photos are shown in this book, which tries to portray a representative selection of Knight's Cross winners and their units. The scope of this book series does not allow comprehensive coverage, and the captions focus on the medals shown and the justification for their awarding. Much of the information I provide is expanded upon in my other books, or in the ones listed for further reading. I have tried to show both the extreme heroism most Waffen-SS Knight's Cross winners displayed, and the darker stories in the background.

Some details didn't fit, and for every photo there was more to tell. When Kurt Meyer is shown smiling with Wilhelm Mohnke, it should be remembered that Meyer destroyed two Ukrainian villages after the death of a friend, and that Mohnke is believed to be responsible for the killing of prisoners in 1940 and 1944. Eberhard Heder had distinguished careers in the Waffen-SS and the postwar Bundeswehr. However, a recent study includes an accusation that during 1941 he was active in looting Jewish possessions in Galicia. I hope that readers will remember that a man can be both a hero and a villain, or can perform heroic actions while serving a bad cause. It should also be realized that while the Knight's Cross winners of the Waffen-SS were in no way victims, their wartime experiences demanded a high price in physical and mental scarring. Some were killed in action after winning their award, and all of them lost friends and comrades in the course of the war. The photos show the high points of their service, but it shouldn't be forgotten that, for all his happiness in his photos in this book, Fritz Witt was torn apart by a naval artillery shell in Normandy.

In my books, I attempt to put a human face on a war whose story is often told through lists, statistics, and simplistic judgements. I also shed light on campaigns that are little-known to English-language readers. It's my hope that readers come away from this book with a new appreciation of the events of the Secord World War. Thanks for reading my work.

Along with thanking the usual suspects, my thanks this time go out to Chris Evans, Andrey Zubkov, Petter Klellander, and Michael Miller. This book is dedicated to the memory of Ember, Ember Bo-bember, my beloved kitty for almost 19 years. It is also dedicated to the memory of Neil Ellwood Peart, who contributed to the soundtrack of my life for decades. Rest in peace, Mitakuye Oyasin.

Marc Rikmenspoel
Denver, Colorado
March 5, 2020

Knight's Cross Winners of the Waffen-SS

The Knight's Cross of the Iron Cross, in its various grades, was the highest German military award for bravery and combat success during the Second World War. The Iron Cross itself dated from 1813, during the Prussian War of Liberation. It was reactivated in 1870 for the Franco-Prussian War, and again in 1914 for the First World War.

The Knight's Cross was a new addition to the Iron Cross, added on September 1, 1939. In previous wars, dating back to the eighteenth century, the Pour le Mérite had been the highest Prussian award for bravery. Its French name reflected the prevailing language of German nobility in the era of its creation. An extension of this is that it was an award for officers and aristocrats. While the Iron Cross and the Pour le Mérite were Prussian decorations, they were awarded throughout the German military, and to their allies, during the First World War.

The Iron Cross was re-activated for issue on the outbreak of the Second World War. The Pour le Mérite was not. In its place, Adolf Hitler decreed the creation of the Knight's Cross of the Iron Cross. This new medal, with a German name, could be awarded to both officers and enlisted men. It recognized both outstanding bravery and successful command of important operations.

The original intention of the German military was to split the Iron Cross awards into four levels. The base was the Iron Cross Second Class, presented for an act of bravery beyond the normal performance of duty. It was the prerequisite for the Iron Cross First Class, which recognized further or more significant bravery. Special clasps were created for both classes, to be presented to men who held the First World War versions of either Iron Cross and won them again in the current war. The Knight's Cross was to be a much rarer decoration, presented for actions decisive to the war effort. Finally, the Grand Cross of the Iron Cross was intended to be the ultimate medal, only awarded a few times to senior leadership. In the event it was awarded just once, to Hermann Göring following the 1940 Western Campaign.

The prolonged war saw German soldiers, sailors and air crew perform multiple acts of bravery. These acts were recognized through the creation of additional awards, both in and out of the Iron Cross series. To the Knight's Cross of the Iron Cross was added, for further decisive bravery or leadership, the Oak Leaves, then the Swords, the Diamonds and finally the Golden Oak Leaves with Swords and Diamonds. This last was awarded just once, and its predecessor only twenty-seven times.

Many members of the German military performed acts of bravery that would have qualified them to win the Iron Cross First Class on multiple occasions. This became recognized through the creation of the German Cross in Gold. The Iron Cross First Class was a prerequisite, but the German Cross in Gold was kept separate from the Knight's Cross and was awarded approximately five times as often. It was not a prerequisite for the Knight's Cross, and many Knight's Cross winners never received the German Cross in Gold, while others earned it after being awarded their Knight's Cross.

On other occasions, acts of overwhelming bravery were performed, but which were of local, more than strategic importance. For this, the recognition came via entry in the Honor Roll of the German Army, Navy, or Air Force. Waffen-SS men were included in the Honor Roll of the German Army, and men entered on the Roll received a special clasp to wear on the ribbon of the Iron Cross Second Class.

The final high award that was discussed in the context of the others was the Close Combat Clasp in Gold. The Close Combat Clasp was created during 1942 to recognize the prolonged time that infantrymen and their supporting services spent on the front lines. While a limited number of "days" could be counted for extended continuous front-line service, the intention was to award the Close Combat Clasp for actual days of hand-to-hand combat with the enemy, as recorded in the recipient's paybook by his superiors. The basic Bronze grade was for fifteen days, while the Silver was for thirty. The Close Combat Clasp in Gold was awarded to men who had engaged in fifty or more days of hand-to-hand combat. As a common but unofficial practice, men who earned the Close Combat Clasp in Gold received an automatic award of the German Cross in Gold, and its prerequisite grades of the Iron Cross if they hadn't yet been awarded these. For men of the Waffen-SS, it was not unusual to see them wearing a combination of Iron Crosses, the German Cross in Gold, the Close Combat Clasp, the Knight's Cross and sometimes the Honor Roll Clasp. 'Assault Badges', which were valued but were less prestigious than any of the above, were also commonly worn by experienced soldiers, along with Wound Badges and a variety of foreign decorations.

The Waffen-SS was the military arm of the Nazi Party. It was a branch of the Schützstaffel (SS), the protection squads formed to guard Nazi speakers at political rallies. The Waffen-SS developed from four primary sources. The most important was the political readiness detachments the SS organized in several German cities after the Nazis came to power in early 1933. By 1935 these detachments became organized along military lines as battalions, and eventually regiments, and were then called SS special-purpose troops (SS-VT). Their mission was to maintain order in the event of anti-Nazi revolutionary activity. By 1938, the SS-VT comprised the regiments Deutschland, Germania and Der Führer, along with supporting battalions of specialists such as signalers and combat engineers. This militarized force was tolerated by the German Army because it freed them from having to worry about quelling civil unrest.

The second source of the Waffen-SS was the SS bodyguard that Adolf Hitler formed after becoming Chancellor of Germany. His Leibstandarte (LAH) developed into an infantry regiment similar to those of the SS-VT. It later expanded into a brigade, and eventually a division.

The SS was in charge of the German concentration camp system. These camps required guards, who were known as Death's Head formations (SS-TV). Guards were recruited far in excess of the numbers required, so that the SS could have another militarized force under its command. The SS-TV also became organized into infantry regiments, though their training remained at a lower level than that of the SS-VT and LAH.

Finally, the SS also became in charge of the German State Police (OP). The Treaty of Versailles limited the German Army to only 100,000 men. The leaders of the army accepted only the most qualified candidates. Other men, only slightly less qualified, were instead channeled into the police forces, so they could maintain paramilitary training and be ready to serve in the army again whenever future expansion occurred. As the SS formed the SS-VT, LAH and SS-TV, police leaders were transferred to serve with them.

The German Army and SS understood that if Germany went to war, the excess men of the SS-TV and OP would be formed into divisions for combat. The outbreak of the Second World War led to discussions in the autumn of 1939. The result was that the SS was allowed to control the new SS-Totenkopf and SS-Polizei divisions. By early 1940, SS military units became known by the umbrella term Waffen-SS.

The SS was already authorized to create additional SS-TV regiments on a wartime basis, for occupation duty in lands conquered during wartime. These "wartime reinforcements" were gradually converted into SS infantry regiments. SS cavalry regiments were formed for similar duties, and gradually expanded in number.

The SS actively recruited non-Germans for both political and military service. Initially, it sought Germans from outside Germany and Austria (Volksdeutsche), and from peoples it considered to be of related Germanic stock. The SS hoped to use its recruits as a wedge to introduce Nazi ideology into other countries. As the Second World War progressed, increasing numbers of foreign men, often not German or Germanic, were brought into SS military service on the basis of wartime need.

While the original mission of the Waffen-SS was homeland security and maintaining order in occupied territories, it was considered appropriate that its units see front-line service. This would give them combat experience and establish credentials for their other roles. At the front, Waffen-SS units fought under German Army command, though at times they could be commandeered for other services, such as aiding police forces in anti-partisan operations and assisting Einsatzgruppen murder squads. Certain units had these tasks as their primary mission, but the majority of the Waffen-SS fought as combat soldiers, seeing action on every front except North Africa. Through their service, the men of the Waffen-SS qualified for the full variety of German military and police decorations. Showing photos of Waffen-SS men wearing the highest of these decorations is the purpose of this book.

The Waffen-SS had limited involvement in the Polish Campaign. LAH saw heavy fighting, especially during the Polish counteroffensive along the Bzura River. Much of the SS-VT served with German Army elements in a mixed Panzer Division. The Germania Regiment served separately, and one of its battalions was mauled by elite Polish troops forcing a passage to Romania and exile. SS-TV and cavalry units were used in murder operations against the Polish population after the occupation. No Knight's Crosses were earned by the Waffen-SS in these military and police operations.

The various parts of the SS-VT were brought together on October 19, 1939 to form the SS-V Division. This was later known as SS-Division Reich, and finally as Das Reich. The Totenkopf and Polizei divisions began to organize around this time. Thus, for the 1940 Western Campaign, the Waffen-SS consisted of three motorized divisions and LAH still at regimental strength.

During the fighting that began on May 10, 1940, LAH and the Der Führer Regiment advanced into the Netherlands. Der Führer distinguished itself by breaking through the Dutch Grebbe Line of defenses in the Grebbe Hills. As Dutch resistance collapsed, LAH and the SS-V Division advanced into Belgium, occupying the strategic area around Antwerp. After further fighting around Dunkirk, they participated in the battle for France which saw the complete German victory.

Totenkopf and the SS-Polizei Division fought their first battles during the Western Campaign. Totenkopf fought in Belgium, defending against the British tank attack at Arras. It was then part of the battle for France, ultimately driving to the Spanish border. The SS-Polizei Division was in reserve during the first phase of the campaign. It was then used as an assault division, despite being a horse-drawn infantry unit, in the battle for France. Neither Totenkopf nor the SS-Polizei Division earned Knight's Crosses during these combats.

LAH commander Sepp Dietrich before the war. He won the first Knight's Cross awarded to a member of the Waffen-SS on July 4, 1940 from a recommendation prepared by German Army Commander-in-Chief Walther von Brauchitsch. It recognized Dietrich's leadership in Poland and the Western Campaign. Dietrich wears his First World War Panzer Assault Badge next to his Iron Cross First Class from the same war. Behind him, on the right, is Blood Flag standard-bearer Jakob Grimminger.

Felix Steiner was awarded the Knight's Cross on August 15, 1940 for his Deutschland Regiment's role in the Western Campaign. Steiner wears the clasps to both of his First World War Iron Crosses.

Der Führer Regiment commander Georg Keppler. He was awarded the third Waffen-SS Knight's Cross on August 22, 1940 for the way his regiment broke through the Dutch Grebbe Line. This considerably hastened the surrender of the Netherlands. Keppler also held both classes of the First World War Iron Cross.

Ludwig Kepplinger was one of Keppler's platoon commanders in the 11th Company of Der Führer. With only two other men, he eliminated several Dutch forts. This made the regiment's advance through the Grebbe Line possible. Kepplinger's Knight's Cross was dated September 4, 1940. By that date he had received a field promotion to Untersturmführer for bravery in the face of the enemy. However, he had probably not had the opportunity to update his dress uniform prior to the taking of this formal portrait. Kepplinger had received five bullet wounds the day after his decisive action, and this is reflected in his Wound Badge in Silver, worn under his Iron Cross First Class.

Fritz Vogt was a noted daredevil in the SS-V Reconnaissance Battalion. Among his platoon's accomplishments was the capture of an entire French battalion during the clearing of the Scheldt estuary. Vogt was the second of three Waffen-SS September 4, 1940 Knight's Cross recipients. He received his decoration from SS-V Division Commander Paul Hausser at a ceremony held in the occupied Netherlands.

The third September 4, 1940 Knight's Cross winner was Fritz Witt, commander of the 1st Battalion of the Deutschland Regiment. He had led his men in close combat against a British tank attack on May 27, 1940. Later, towards the close of the campaign, Witt's battalion captured almost 20,000 French prisoners. In this photo, Witt wears Deutschland's "SS 1" collar patch that was officially discontinued in the late spring of 1940.

The Balkans Campaign was a bit of a sideshow for the German military. Only LAH and the SS-V Division, now retitled SS-Division Reich, participated. LAH followed the Panzer advance through Serbia before going into action to force open the passes of northern Greece. Once in southern Greece, elements of LAH made a surprise crossing of the Gulf of Corinth, which outflanked Allied defenses in the Peloponnese.

Reich passed through the Serbian portion of the Banat, as part of the German operation to capture Belgrade. The city surrendered to a reconnaissance patrol from the division. This was a propaganda coup for the Waffen-SS, as German Army units had been in more favorable positions to take the Yugoslav capital.

Preparations for the planned invasion of the Soviet Union continued during the fighting in Greece and Yugoslavia. The Waffen-SS assembled a new motorized division by merging the Germania Regiment (detached from Reich) with newly-formed infantry regiments created to include Scandinavian and Dutch-Flemish volunteers, titled Nordland and Westland. Together they became the Wiking Division, which was supposed to attain the same elite status as LAH and Reich. SS infantry regiments, retitled from the Totenkopf regiments, continued occupation duties. The exception was SS-Infantry Regiment 11, which had joined Reich as the replacement for Germania.

Fritz Klingenberg led an advance patrol of ten men from his 1st Company of Motorcycle Battalion Reich into Belgrade on April 12, 1941. He met German diplomats by chance, and was brought to the German Consulate. The mayor of the city came to the consulate for a discussion. Klingenberg bluffed that he had many more men with him, a short distance away. The mayor took the bait, and surrendered the city to Klingenberg. This feat brought Klingenberg the Knight's Cross on April 14.

Klingenberg received his Knight's Cross soon after, in a personal audience with Adolf Hitler.

Fritz Witt was transferred to LAH prior to the Balkans Campaign. He commanded the 1st Battalion, with Gerd Pleiss commanding its 1st Company. On April 12, the same day Klingenberg captured Belgrade, Pleiss led the decisive attack that enabled the Germans to capture the Klidi Pass in northern Greece. For this, Pleiss was awarded the Knight's Cross a week later on April 20. Pleiss was a tall man, and his company contained the tallest men in the LAH, each at least 190cm in height. Pleiss is seen here on home leave, prior to the start of the campaign in the Soviet Union.

Kurt Meyer commanded the LAH Reconnaissance Battalion during the Balkans Campaign, and won the Knight's Cross on May 18, 1941. His unit had broken Greek resistance around Klissura Pass, and captured many prisoners. This photo was taken a few months later, during LAH's advance through the southern Soviet Union.

Germany invaded the Soviet Union on June 22, 1941 in Operation BARBAROSSA. For the offensive, the Waffen-SS contributed LAH, Reich, Totenkopf, SS-Polizei, Wiking and units formed from former Totenkopf regiments. These included three regiments in Finland (two of them forming SS-Battle Group Nord, later expanded into a mountain division), a brigade of cavalry and two infantry brigades. These cavalry and infantry brigades were formed to assist the Action Groups in murdering civilians and stragglers, but after serving in this role during the summer, gradually took on combat duties due to the crises of the fall and winter.

LAH and Wiking fought with Army Group South during this campaign. Reich was with Army Group Center. Army Group North included Totenkopf and SS-Polizei. All saw extremely heavy fighting and took serious casualties. The summer and fall were times of advances, sometimes mixed with defensive stands. The winter featured successful defensive fighting against Soviet counteroffensives. The Waffen-SS units were depleted, so that LAH and Reich were withdrawn to rebuild, followed eventually by Totenkopf. SS-Polizei and Wiking remained at the front all through 1942, with the former continuing to fight defensive battles and the latter advancing to the Caucasus. By the end of 1942, the German Eastern Front was facing a new round of crises. LAH, Reich (now with its title modified to Das Reich) and Totenkopf were joined into the SS-Panzerkorps. Battle Group Nord and the SS-Cavalry Brigade had transformed into full divisions, and a division of ethnic German conscripts was preparing to enter combat in occupied Yugoslavia as SS-Volunteer Mountain Division Prinz Eugen. The forming of new SS armored divisions was in the planning stage.

From this point onward, it is no longer possible to offer comprehensive coverage of Waffen-SS Knight's Cross winners. The photos will focus on images with many medals visible, and on ones portraying leading personalities.

Theodor Wisch commanded the 2nd Battalion of LAH during BARBAROSSA. During the second week of July, he and his men defended the main supply routes of Army Group South. For this, Wisch was awarded the Knight's Cross on September 15, 1941. Soon after, he posed with the other LAH Knight's Cross winners. From the left are Gerd Pleiss (died of wounds on November 17, 1941), Wisch, Sepp Dietrich, Fritz Witt and Kurt Meyer.

Paul Hausser was the first commander of the Reich Division and later of the SS-Panzerkorps. His distinguished leadership of Reich in the Western Campaign and then during the advance to Yelna, in Russia, was recognized through his August 8, 1941 award of the Knight's Cross. Hausser wears the early style of Gruppenführer collar patches in this photo taken soon after he received his Knight's Cross. Two months later, on October 14, Hausser was wounded by shrapnel in his face, losing his right eye. For the rest of the war, he was usually photographed from the left side.

Totenkopf Division commander Theodor Eicke in the summer or autumn of 1942. He won the Knight's Cross on December 26, 1941 for his division's leading role in containing Soviet counterattacks during Army Group North's advance towards Leningrad and Novgorod. These were considered incredibly difficult and costly battles, but Totenkopf experienced far worse in early 1942 at Staraya Russa and then at Demyansk. For these, Eicke was awarded the Oak Leaves on April 20, 1942, with his promotion to Obergruppenführer dated the same day. In this image, Eicke also wears his Wound Badge in Silver and Gold Nazi Party Badge. Nazi Party members in the Wehrmacht and Waffen-SS had their memberships suspended for the duration of the war, since soldiers were not supposed to be political. However, Waffen-SS members sometimes wore their Nazi Party badges for propaganda photos such as this one, which would be distributed to the press.

Seen in the spring of 1942 is SS-Polizei Division commander Alfred Wünnenberg. His Knight's Cross was won on November 15, 1941 as a regimental commander in the same division. The SS-Polizei was not motorized at this time, but had fought with distinction as an assault division in the advance on Leningrad. Wünnenberg wears Clasps to both of his Iron Crosses won in the First World War. Also from that conflict, he displays the Wound Badge in Silver and the Bavarian Observer's Badge for Pilots. Next to the latter are SS runes showing SS membership while wearing a police general's tunic. Unusually, the tunic has a Heer eagle on the left sleeve instead of the typical SS pattern. Wünnenberg won the Oak Leaves on April 23, 1942 after his division played a leading role in containing the Soviet Volkhov Pocket.

Wünnenberg wears an SS tunic and his Oak Leaves in this early October 1942 portrait. SS-Polizei held an awards ceremony that day, honoring two Knight's Cross winners and two German Cross in Gold winners. From the left are Günther Butte (German Cross in Gold September 11, 1942), Karl Schümers (German Cross in Gold August 3, 1942, Knight's Cross September 30, 1942), Wünnenberg, Otto Gieseke (German Cross in Gold September 12, 1942, Knight's Cross September 30, 1942), and Hans Traupe (German Cross in Gold September 25, 1942). These newly-decorated officers had distinguished themselves in the fighting for the Volkhov Pocket and during the First Battle of Lake Ladoga. Traupe later won the Knight's Cross on February 23, 1944 for his battalion's role in covering the German retreat from the Volkhov River to the Panther Line defenses the previous month.

Rudolf Seitz was an experienced gun commander in the SS-Polizei Anti-Tank Battalion. He was awarded the Knight's Cross on October 21, 1942, probably for actions during the First Battle of Lake Ladoga. Seitz's veteran status is shown by his Wound Badge in Silver and General Assault Badge (awarded to personnel who were not in the infantry or armor branches of service). He also has the ribbon for the Eastern Front Medal under the ribbon for his Iron Cross Second Class.

August Zingel distinguished himself leading raids and reconnaissance missions in the Demyansk cauldron. A successful operation on September 10, 1942 was the catalyst for his award of the Knight's Cross a few weeks later on October 4. Zingel's dress uniform includes an Honor Stripe on his right sleeve for his early Hitler Youth membership, and the Infantry Assault Badge next to his Iron Cross First Class.

Seitz and Zingel posed together for this photo, taken during 1943. Both became officers the next year. Zingel wears the Death's Head cuff title unofficially used by Totenkopf Infanterie Regiment 1 (later known as SS-Panzergrenadier Regiment 5 Totenkopf), and has his regiment's "1" on his shoulder boards.

Karl Ullrich took command of Totenkopf's Combat Engineer Battalion just before BARBAROSSA. In early 1942, he led a battle group based around his battalion. It held a key strongpoint near Staraya Russa for several weeks against intense Soviet attacks, for which Ullrich won the Knight's Cross on February 14, 1942. The scar on his chin was not obtained in combat, but was actually from a pre-war injury.

Ludwig Köchle led many raids and counterattacks during Totenkopf's early 1942 defensive fighting around Staraya Russa. This brought him the Knight's Cross on February 28, 1942. Köchle was featured in many press photos such as this one, but was only able to enjoy his award for three months. He was killed by Soviet artillery fire on June 9, in the Demyansk cauldron.

An important part of Totenkopf's early defensive success at Demyansk was the support provided by its assault gun battery. For this, the battery's acting commander, Erwin Meierdress, was awarded the Knight's Cross on March 13, 1942. He received the award while hospitalized and other photos from this sequence show that he was wearing pajama pants while posing.

Another Totenkopf hero from this era was Hans Hirning, who won his Knight's Cross on October 23, 1942. He had been part of the veteran cadre that enabled the division to keep fighting at Demyansk, with mostly replacements in the ranks. Along with his Iron Cross First Class, Infantry Assault Badge and Wound Badge in Black, Hirning has on his right sleeve the Tank Destruction Badge for single-handedly destroying an enemy tank or armored vehicle.

Helmut Pförtner was considered one of the bravest officers in Wiking during the summer of 1941. His actions brought him both the German Cross in Gold and the Knight's Cross on November 22, 1941. He was hospitalized due to wounds on that date, and in this spring 1942 photo he wears the Wound Badge in Silver next to his Infantry Assault Badge in Silver.

Pförtner's battalion commander was August Dieckmann, who led Germania's 1st Battalion in defensive fighting detached from Wiking in early 1942. German Army commanders recommended him for the Knight's Cross, which was awarded on April 23, 1942.

The guns of Karl Schlamelcher's 3rd Battalion of the Wiking Artillery Regiment provided outstanding support during the Mius River fighting in early 1942. This brought him the Knight's Cross on March 1 of that year. Schlamelcher was badly wounded that summer, during the advance to the Caucasus. This earned him the Wound Badge in Silver that he wears in this photo. No longer fit for front-line service, Schlamelcher excelled in commanding artillery instructional units for the rest of the war. He never fully recovered from his injuries, and died in 1948 at the age of 35.

Bernhard Griese and Rudolf Pannier pose together during a meeting with Heinrich Himmler, circa late May 1942. Though not obvious from this photo, the men were the same age, both born in 1897. Both were First World War veterans, who then served in the paramilitary Freikorps before making careers in the Order Police. Griese won the Knight's Cross on May 3, 1942 for leading Police Battalion 323 in defensive fighting west of Moscow in the preceding months. He wears the Clasp to his First World War Iron Cross Second Class on the ribbon to the earlier award, along with the Second World War Iron Cross First Class. Pannier won the Knight's Cross on May 11, 1942 for commanding the 1st Battalion of Police Infantry Regiment 2 in the SS-Polizei Division in holding the key strongpoint of Ljubino Pole during the early stages of the Volkhov Pocket fighting.

SS-Infantry Regiment 4 was nearly destroyed in the defensive fighting west of Moscow in early 1942. Its sacrifice brought it the honor title Langemarck, with Commander Hinrich Schuldt winning the Knight's Cross on April 5, 1942. Schuldt, nicknamed "Kapitän" from his earlier service as a naval officer, is seen a few months later, posing with his 1st Battalion commander, Jakob 'Jopp' Fick.

The countries allied with Germany occasionally bestowed decorations on Waffen-SS men who fought near their territory or with their soldiers. LAH rested and reorganized during the summer and autumn of 1942, and Fritz Witt posed at this time to display his new, foreign acquisitions. Under his Knight's Cross is the Romanian Order of the Star, while the Bulgarian Military Order for Bravery in War is below his Iron Cross First Class. Witt also wears the German Cross in Gold he won on February 8 1942.

The SS-Panzerkorps, with LAH, Das Reich and Totenkopf, returned to combat in January 1943. After LAH and Das Reich defended near Kharkov and eventually abandoned the city, they were joined by Totenkopf in a successful counteroffensive. Kharkov was recaptured, and the Soviet winter offensive that had started around Stalingrad was ended.

At the same time, Wiking retreated from the Caucasus before helping contain the Soviet winter offensive to the south of Kharkov. SS-Polizei and the 2nd SS-Infantry Brigade (now an international unit, including Germanic and Baltic volunteers) fought near Leningrad in the Second Battle of Lake Ladoga. The foreign volunteers then spent the summer of 1943 reorganizing into independent brigades and divisions of Dutch, Flemish, Walloons, Scandinavians, Estonians and Latvians.

The SS-Panzerkorps had a lead role in the early July 1943 Kursk offensive. LAH was then sent to Italy to prop up the Fascist government. Das Reich and Totenkopf joined German Army units in destroying the Soviet Mius River bridgehead at the end of July and beginning of August. They then returned to the Kharkov area, with the city being lost for good in late summer. As this went on, Wiking contained a major Soviet offensive near Izyum, before joining Das Reich and Totenkopf in the unsuccessful defense of the Kharkov area. All three divisions then helped cover the German retreat to the Dnieper River.

The Soviets advanced across the Dnieper at several points and recaptured Kiev on November 6. LAH returned to Ukraine during October, where it was nearly destroyed over the following six months. Totenkopf was also reduced to remnants as it gradually retreated from southern Ukraine to eastern Romania. The majority of Das Reich was withdrawn in early December, 1943 for rebuilding. The battlegroup it left behind fought in Ukraine until the spring, when the last depleted elements rejoined the main body.

Wiking was surrounded in the Cherkassy Pocket in early 1944, along with the attached Walloon Assault Brigade and German Army units. The encircled troops broke out during February, with heavy casualties and the loss of most equipment. Wiking then refitted, while elements fought near Kovel. Totenkopf rebuilt in Romania. LAH refitted in Flanders, near its newly-formed sister division, Hitlerjugend. Das Reich rebuilt in France, near the newly-formed Götz von Berlichingen Division.

The new Hohenstaufen and Frundsberg Divisions formed in France and Belgium at the same time, but were committed to combat ahead of the other new divisions. During March 1944, grouped as the 2nd SS-Panzerkorps, they were sent to western Ukraine to relieve the German troops, including elements of LAH and the Das Reich battlegroup, caught in the Hube Pocket. After this successful operation, Hohenstaufen and Frundsberg were kept at readiness for a return to France for their originally-intended role, combating the Allied invasion expected in the summer of 1944.

Gerardus Mooyman was the gunner of an anti-tank gun in the Anti-Tank Company of the Legion Nederland. He knocked out numerous Soviet tanks during the Second Battle of Lake Ladoga, for which he won the Knight's Cross on February 20, 1943. Mooyman's achievement was honored at a banquet, where he sat by 2nd SS-Infantry Brigade commander Fritz von Scholz. The latter had won his Knight's Cross on January 18, 1942 as commander of the Nordland Regiment in Wiking. Soon after this photo was taken, he began forming the Nordland Division, which had his old regiment as cadre.

Hinrich Schuldt in the late summer of 1943, as commander of the 2nd SS-Infantry Brigade, which was now a Latvian unit. Schuldt had won the Oak Leaves on April 2 of that year, after commanding a mixed battlegroup for emergency service on the Don River front during the Stalingrad crisis. Three weeks later, on April 21, he won the German Cross in Gold for unspecified actions in the preceding years. Schuldt has also added the Wound Badge in Silver after being seriously wounded during the Don fighting.

Another early 1943 Oak Leaves winner was Fritz Witt. His award was dated March 1, and reflected 1941 combats in Greece and the Soviet Union and early 1943 defensive fighting near Kharkov. Witt soon left LAH, to begin forming its intended sister division, Hitlerjugend.

Also assigned to the cadre of Hitlerjugend was Kurt Meyer, who led one of its infantry regiments. He too won the Oak Leaves during the Kharkov campaign on February 23 in recognition of successful actions in 1941 and early 1943. Despite the serious situation at the front, he was flown to Hitler's headquarters to receive the award personally, as shown in this photo. Two days later, Meyer was back with his LAH Reconnaissance Battalion in Ukraine. It was only learned many years after the war that during the February fighting, Meyer had his men destroy two Ukrainian villages and kill hundreds of civilians in retaliation for alleged partisan activity.

Meyer poses in the late spring of 1943 with Max Wünsche, commander of the 1st Battalion of SS-Panzer Regiment 1. Wünsche won the Knight's Cross on February 28, 1943, three days after he had been awarded the German Cross in Gold. His battalion had frequently fought alongside Meyer's during the defensive fighting near Kharkov, prior to the German counter-offensive. Wünsche also became part of the Hitlerjugend cadre, serving as the first commander of the division's Panzer Regiment.

Meyer was known for recommending his subordinates for decorations. Here he places the ribbon of the Knight's Cross under the collar of Hermann Weiser, his 2nd Company commander. Weiser's award was dated March 28, 1943 and reflected his leading role in the recapture of Valki that month, as well as how his company held out successfully while surrounded during the recapture of Kharkov. LAH divisional Surgeon Dr Hermann Besuden watches on the right.

Sepp Dietrich's 51st birthday on May 28, 1943 was celebrated with a big banquet in Kharkov, which was attended by many Waffen-SS senior officers. A less formal photo from this occasion finds Kurt Meyer sharing a toast with Wilhelm Mohnke, commander of LAH Replacement Battalion.

Another photo from the same event. Dietrich poses with Teddy Wisch behind him. Flanking them are recent Knight's Cross winners Hugo Kraas, left (March 23, 1943 as commander of the 1st Battalion, SS-Panzergrenadier Regiment 2), and Albert Frey (March 3, 1943 as commander of the 1st Battalion, SS-Panzergrenadier Regiment 1). For this occasion, Dietrich wears the ribbon of the Blood Order on his right pocket flap and his Gold Nazi Party Badge on the left flap. Instead of his First World War Iron Cross 1st Class with Second World War Clasp, he has on his left pocket his First World War Tank Battle Badge, and his honorary Luftwaffe Combined Pilot-Observer's Badge in Gold.

Rudolf Sandig distinguished himself on several occasions during the Kharkov campaign while commanding the 2nd Battalion of SS-Panzergrenadier Regiment 2. This led to his Knight's Cross, dated May 5, 1943. Sandig had won one of the first German Crosses in Gold awarded in the German military on December 26, 1941. As with other LAH officers, just visible below his Iron Cross First Class, he has the Bulgarian Military Order for Bravery in War.

LAH armored half-track battalion, under the command of Joachim Peiper, led the division's advance into Kharkov. Twice it captured bridgeheads which acted as the springboard for other divisional elements to carry the offensive forward. For this, and for the earlier rescue of the trapped 320th Infantry Division, Peiper won the Knight's Cross on March 12, 1943. At the same time, his platoon commanders Werner Wolff and Paul Guhl were awarded the Iron Cross First Class.

During the recapture of Kharkov, Walter Gerth's 7th Battery of SS-Artillery Regiment 3 found itself blocking the retreat route of surrounded Soviet forces. Gerth led his men in heavy combat, which sometimes became hand-to-hand. Their successful stand allowed other elements of Totenkopf to destroy the surrounded Red Army units. Gerth was awarded the Knight's Cross on March 31, 1943. In this photo, he wears the Wound Badge in Gold beneath his binoculars.

Joachim Schubach, the commander of the 3rd Battalion of SS-Panzergrenadier Regiment 5, won his Knight's Cross in circumstances similar to Gerth's. Schubach's command blocked the way of Soviet forces retreating from Kharkov to the south-east, so that they too could be destroyed. Schubach was badly wounded in the fighting on March 17, 1943, and was recommended for the Knight's Cross the same day. The award was approved on April 3.

Also awarded the Knight's Cross on April 3, 1943 was Arzelino 'Lino' Masarie, acting commander of Totenkopf's Reconnaissance Battalion. During the drive to retake Kharkov, he had captured and held an important village on his own initiative. This had kept the offensive moving forward and resulted in extensive booty. Masarie was one of a number of SS men with Italian ancestry who won the Knight's Cross.

Totenkopf was hard-pressed to hold the villages it had captured during the retaking of Kharkov. It successfully fought off numerous Soviet counterattacks, and Waldemar Riefkogel distinguished himself in one of these engagements. On March 17, 1943 he led two tanks of his 1st Company of SS-Panzer Regiment 3 in supporting the infantry holding the village of Tschugujev. After knocking out several Soviet tanks, Riefkogel dismounted and led the infantry in an attack that routed their opponent. He was recommended for the Knight's Cross soon after, but the award was not approved until July 11, 1943 during the Kursk offensive.

Das Reich held an award ceremony during April 1943 for men who had won the Knight's Cross or German Cross in Gold. New division commander Walter Krüger is placing the ribbon of the Knight's Cross around the neck of Hans Weiss. Vinzenz Kaiser stands next to Weiss, with four Tank Destruction Badges on his right sleeve. Behind Kaiser, divisional Adjutant Dieter Kesten is adjusting the Knight's Cross ribbon under the collar of Sylvester Stadler. Finally, Karl Heinz Worthmann is next to Stadler, in black Panzer uniform.

Karl Heinz Worthmann was a career NCO with Germania, as reflected by his Infantry Assault Badge. His Silver Wound Badge was due to being severely wounded during Barbarossa. Upon recovery, Worthmann became a platoon commander in the 6th Company of SS-Panzer Regiment 2. He led numerous decisive counterattacks during the defensive fighting near Kharkov in early February 1943. On February 20, Worthmann was both promoted to junior officer for bravery, and recommended for the Knight's Cross. The award was approved on March 31.

Sylvester Stadler owed his unusual first name to having been born on December 30, the time known as the Sylvester New Year's holiday in Central Europe. As commander of the 2nd Battalion of Der Führer, his Knight's Cross was approved on April 6, 1943 for leading an important night attack during the advance to recapture Kharkov.

Also approved on April 6 was the Knight's Cross for Vinzenz Kaiser. He had taken acting command of the 3rd Battalion of Der Führer during the Kharkov campaign. He led a decisive attack on his own initiative during the recapture of Kharkov, and personally destroyed four Soviet tanks. This is shown by the four Tank Destruction Badges on his right sleeve. Kaiser wears the Gold Nazi Party Badge above his Iron Cross First Class. As mentioned before, soldiers were supposed to be apolitical, so Waffen-SS men who were Nazi Party members had their memberships suspended for the duration of the war. However, individuals such as Kaiser still wore their Party badges for official portraits to show their affiliation.

Hans Weiss was acting commander of Das Reich's Reconnaissance Battalion during the Kharkov counteroffensive. He was another April 6 Knight's Cross winner for personally leading the advance element of his battalion in several crucial actions during the drive toward Kharkov, and then in the city. During 1943, Weiss transferred to command of the 1st Battalion of SS-Panzer Regiment 2. This 1944 photo shows him in Panzer uniform, with the German Cross in Gold he won on April 23 of that year. Weiss also wears the Wound Badge in Silver and the Close Combat Clasp in Silver, an award not listed among his decorations received.

Also at Das Reich's awards ceremony were Otto Kumm and Christian Tychsen, the latter overcome with emotion. Kumm received the certificate for the Oak Leaves to his Knight's Cross. Tychsen was awarded the Knight's Cross on March 31, 1943 as the commander of the 2nd Battalion of SS-Panzer Regiment 2. He had led attacks the previous month which relieved pressure on Das Reich, enabling the division to extricate itself from Kharkov and retreat successfully prior to the counteroffensive that recaptured the city.

Der Führer commander Otto Kumm was the first Oak Leaves winner in Das Reich, with his award approved on April 6. He had always been up front at the most important point of his regiment's commitment area, as it parried Soviet attacks and launched counterattacks. This had delayed the Soviet advance on Kharkov during early February 1943. Kumm received his Oak Leaves personally from Adolf Hitler at the latter's headquarters on May 20, 1943.

Not part of the assembled award winners was Hans Macher, commander of Deutschland's Combat Engineer Company. He was on a propaganda tour in Germany with other veterans of the victorious Kharkov campaign and received his Knight's Cross there. It was approved on April 3, for the way he and his company led Deutschland's advance into Kharkov during the recapture of the city. As a Combat Engineer, Macher wears the General Assault Badge next to his Wound Badge in Silver. His Tank Destruction Badge was for a Soviet tank he destroyed on February 24, 1943.

Karl Kloskowski was an NCO platoon commander in the 4th Company of SS-Panzer Regiment 2. He led the Das Reich advance on Pavlograd on February 21, 1943. His point platoon captured an important bridge, which made the conquest of the city possible, and for this he won a delayed award of the Knight's Cross on July 11, 1943. He was also promoted to officer rank.

On July 8, 1943, during the Kursk offensive, as LAH advanced to the north, Franz Staudegger remained in the rear at a maintenance facility with his broken-down Tiger tank. Nearby infantry warned Staudegger that a surprise mass Soviet tank attack was forming to assault their position, and thus strike the flank of the SS-Panzerkorps advance to the north. Staudegger made his Tiger provisionally mobile and moved it to an ambush position. He then defeated the Soviet attack by knocking out twenty-two of their tanks. Staudegger was awarded the Knight's Cross on July 10, and soon after was flown to Hitler's headquarters to report on conditions at the front.

The most famous part of the Battle of Kursk was the 5th Guards Tank Army's attack against LAH on July 12, near Prochorovka. It struck the positions of the battlegroup formed from the half-track battalion and the 2nd Battalion of the Panzer Regiment. A major role in defeating the onslaught was played by the 6th Company of the latter, under the acting command of Rudolf von Ribbentrop, the son of German Foreign Minister Joachim von Ribbentrop. Rudolf von Ribbentrop was awarded the Knight's Cross three days later. He was the last surviving Waffen-SS Knight's Cross winner, until he died on May 20, 2019.

Von Ribbentrop's battalion commander, Martin Gross, won the Knight's Cross on July 22 for the same fighting. He had been awarded the German Cross in Gold following the Kharkov campaign.

Werner Wolff was the adjutant of LAH half-track battalion during Kursk. On July 12, in the Prochorovka fighting, he took acting command of one of his battalion's companies after its commander was wounded. Wolff led the men in destroying many Soviet tanks in close combat. He poses here with the Knight's Cross he was awarded on August 7, 1943 and a Tank Destruction Badge under his adjutant's cords. Wolff also wears the Iron Cross First Class, the Infantry Assault Badge in Bronze, the Wound Badge in Black and the Close Combat Clasp in Bronze.

The lightly-armored Marder tank-destroyers of SS-Panzerjäger Battalion LAH also helped defeat the Soviet attacks on July 12. For this, platoon commander Kurt Sametreiter was awarded the Knight's Cross on July 31. This photo shows him later, after he was promoted to officer rank and transferred to the Panzer Regiment. Sametreiter has LAH ciphers on his shoulder boards, and the Panzer Assault Badge in Silver next to his Iron Cross First Class.

Wiking was in reserve during Kursk. On July 17, it was rushed to the Izyum area, where the Soviets had formed a bridgehead across the Donets River. Over the next four days, the division helped contain repeated Soviet efforts to break out of the bridgehead and cut the main German supply railroad line. Germania commander Jürgen Wagner was awarded the Knight's Cross on July 24 because he was always at the focal point as his regiment helped master the crises of the preceding days.

Albert Müller commanded the anti-tank gun platoon in the 4th Company of Westland. His guns were crucial in helping his battalion hold on to the town of Ssredni, and Müller probably took acting command of his company when the commander was killed in the fighting. Müller was awarded the Knight's Cross on August 4. For this portrait, he wears the uncommon Infantry Assault Badge in Bronze, which he received before Wiking's infantry were reclassified from motorized infantry to Panzergrenadiers.

Also awarded the Knight's Cross on August 4 was Walter Schmidt, commander of Westland's 2nd Battalion. While his battalion held Savodskoje, next to Ssredni, in desperate combat, he led a small group of men across the Donets into the Soviet rear. Their surprise attack eased the pressure against the main body of his battalion.

Günther Sitter was awarded his Knight's Cross a bit later on September 12 for the same fighting. He commanded Westland's 1st Battalion, and thus was Albert Müller's battalion commander. He led the successful defense of Ssredni, to which Müller had made an important contribution. Other photos from this sequence suggest Wiking commander Herbert Otto Gille used his own Knight's Cross as a presentation piece for Sitter.

On the right is Günther-Eberhard Wisliceny, commander of the 3rd Battalion of Regiment Deutschland, posing with his 10th Company commander Helmuth Schreiber. Both men were awarded the Knight's Cross on July 30, 1943 for their leadership in the early phases of the Kursk offensive. Wisliceny wears enlisted-grade collar patches with his officer rank pips, while Schreiber has the normal officer-grade collar patches with laced borders.

A Das Reich command conference in the late summer of 1943. Division commander Walter Krüger is at center, surrounded by his regimental commanders. From the left are SS-Panzer Regiment 2 commander Hans-Albin Freiherr von Reitzenstein, Deutschland commander Heinz Harmel, Krüger, an orderly officer, and Der Führer commander Sylvester Stadler.

Heinz Harmel in the spring of 1944, with the decorations he mostly earned during 1943. He won the Oak Leaves on September 7, 1943 and the Close Combat Clasp in Silver three days later. The Oak Leaves were for Regiment Deutschland's role in the destruction of the Soviet bridgehead on the west bank of the Mius River. Harmel had won one of the first German Crosses in Gold in late 1941, and was awarded his Tank Destruction Badge on the same day as his Knight's Cross, March 31, 1943.

On September 26, 1943, Sylvester Stadler and Walter Krüger flew to Hitler's headquarters to receive the Oak Leaves to their Knight's Crosses. Krüger and Heinrich Himmler observe, as Stadler shakes Hitler's hand. During defensive fighting near Kharkov, Stadler had arrived at a threatened sector ahead of his regiment. With only a handful of men, he held up a Soviet attack while personally manning a machine gun. This brought him the Oak Leaves, awarded on September 16.

Krüger's Oak Leaves were awarded on August 31. They recognized Das Reich's success at Kursk and the Mius bridgehead. On his left breast pocket, Krüger wears the Baltic Cross he earned fighting with the Freikorps in the Baltic States following the First World War.

Josef 'Sepp' Lainer, a platoon commander in the 3rd Company of Der Führer, was awarded the Knight's Cross on October 8, 1943. It was in recognition of his role in the same defensive fighting that had commenced with his regimental commander Stadler's personal action. The medal was presented some time later, along with two decorations awarded on October 15, the Wound Badge in Gold and Close Combat Clasp in Gold. The latter was one of the first to be earned in the German military. In this photo, Lainer also wears the Infantry Assault Badge in Bronze.

Lainer poses with his fellow Tyrolean Johan Thaler, who had won the Knight's Cross on August 14, 1943. Thaler was the driver of a Panzer IV in the 6th Company of SS-Panzer Regiment 2. During the Kursk fighting, in the middle of an armored battle, his tank was hit and made immobile. With great personal effort, Thaler made a temporary fix to the transmission, which made the tank mobile again. It then contributed to the successful outcome of the engagement.

During the second week of November, 1943, Alfred Siegling from SS-Armored Reconnaissance Battalion 2 led a patrol of three armored cars back and forth through no man's land near Zhitomir in Ukraine. The patrol located elements out of contact with their parent formation, and provided constant reports to higher headquarters about the advance of Soviet units. This success, under dangerous circumstances, brought Siegling the award of the Knight's Cross on December 2, 1943. A few days later, the medal was actually presented to Siegling by Das Reich commander Walter Krüger.

Christian Tychsen led the 2nd Battalion of SS-Panzer Regiment 2 with distinction at Kursk, the Mius, and in the retreat to the Dnieper River. His Oak Leaves recommendation mentions these in passing, but cites a decisive counterattack he led on November 1, 1943 as the primary reason he deserved the award. It was approved on December 10, and personally presented by Adolf Hitler at a later date. Observing on the right is Hitler's adjutant Fritz Darges, who later won the Knight's Cross commanding SS-Panzer Regiment 5.

Karl Ullrich poses with Hellmuth Becker after the latter was awarded the Knight's Cross on September 7, 1943. Becker was then commanding SS-Panzergrenadier Regiment 6, which carried the honor title Theodor Eicke, following Eicke's death in the Kharkov campaign. Becker had led his regiment in several successful counterattacks during the August 1943 defensive fighting near Kharkov.

Erwin Meierdress won the Oak Leaves on October 5, 1943 and received them personally from Adolf Hitler. The award recognized his leadership of the 1st Battalion of SS-Panzer Regiment 3 during the recapture of Kharkov, at Kursk, at the Mius bridgehead, and in the August 1943 defensive fighting near Kharkov.

Meierdress posed for multiple portraits after receiving his Oak Leaves. In this one, he wears a conventional grey tunic. Meierdress won the Wound Badge in Gold, and while the date of the award isn't known, he appears to be wearing it here.

Meierdress also posed in his black Panzer tunic, while wearing the same cap for both photos.

Rudolf Säumenicht commanded the 2nd Company in Meierdress's battalion. Säumenicht took acting command of the battalion after Meierdress was wounded, and won the Knight's Cross on October 13, 1943 due to the unit knocking out numerous Soviet tanks while being well below full strength. He wears the Hitler Youth Honor Badge in Gold next to his Iron Cross First Class.

Erich Zepper took acting command of the 2nd Company of the Westland Regiment during the autumn 1943 fighting along the Dnieper, and won the Knight's Cross for this on December 2. Zepper was a career NCO, but this photo is from after he was promoted to junior officer in the spring of 1944.

Similarly to Zepper, Gustav Schreiber was a career NCO in the 7th Company of the Germania Regiment, who took acting command during the late summer and autumn fighting. Schreiber also won the Knight's Cross on December 2, 1943 and five days later was awarded the Close Combat Clasp in Gold. He wears both for this propaganda photo taken soon after.

Teddy Wisch took command of LAH just before the Kursk offensive. Sepp Dietrich left to begin forming the 1st SS-Panzerkorps in Belgium. Dietrich returned to the east late in 1943, paying a visit to his old division beginning on December 2. During this visit are, from the left, Wisch, LAH Chief of Staff Rudolf Lehmann, Dietrich and Hermann Weiser. The latter was now Dietrich's adjutant and escort officer.

Joachim Peiper took command of SS-Panzer Regiment 1 on November 20, 1943 following the death of Georg Schönberger earlier that day. In this new post, Peiper was awarded the Oak Leaves on January 27, 1944. Once the news was received, he posed for this propaganda photo, which then had the Oak Leaves added.

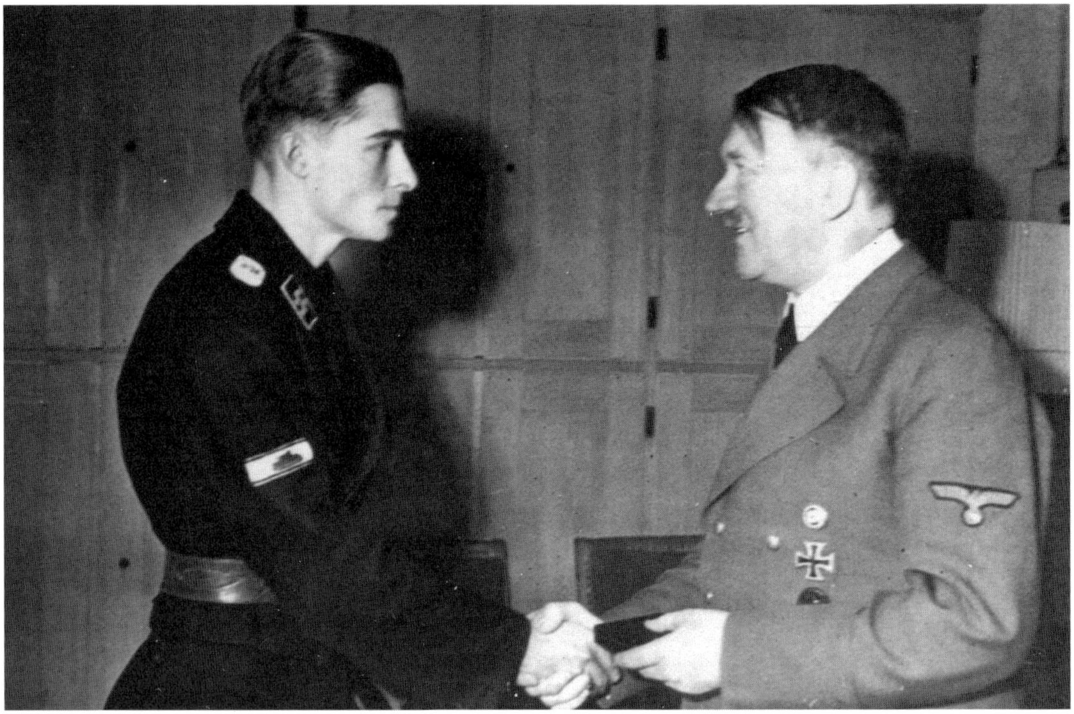

Peiper actually received his Oak Leaves around February 2 in a personal meeting with Hitler. Peiper then went on leave, suffering from exhaustion. His Tank Destruction Badge, earned at Kursk, stands out on the black Panzer uniform.

With Peiper on leave, his 1st Battalion commander, Herbert Kuhlmann, commanded the remnants of SS-Panzer Regiment 1. Kuhlmann was awarded the Knight's Cross on February 13, 1944 for the attacks he had led in the first days of the year.

The Tiger tanks of the 13th Company of SS-Panzer Regiment 1 knocked out numerous Soviet tanks during late 1943 and early the next year. The company was heavily decorated as its reward. The leading ace was Michael Wittmann, awarded the Knight's Cross on January 14, 1944. This photo is from a few days later, when Teddy Wisch presented the Knight's Cross, awarded on January 16, to Wittmann's gunner Balthasar "Bobby" Woll.

When Wittmann went on leave, Helmut Wendorff, known to his comrades as "Bubi" and "Axel", commanded the last Tigers of the 13th Company. Wendorff was awarded the Knight's Cross on February 12, 1944. He has metal LAH ciphers on his shoulder boards.

Bobby Woll was famous among his comrades for his amazing accuracy as a gunner. This portrait is carefully posed to show his medals, his Adolf Hitler cuff title and LAH cipher on his shoulder board.

Wittmann and Woll continued to score many destroyed enemy tanks after their awards. Wittmann was awarded the Oak Leaves remarkably soon after his Knight's Cross, on January 30, 1944. He received them personally from Hitler, and then went on leave. Wittmann married his fiancée Hildegard on March 1 of that year.

In the midst of the many decorations to LAH tankers, division commander Teddy Wisch was awarded the Oak Leaves on February 12, 1944. He posed for this informal portrait in Belgium three months later, while his division was rebuilding.

Heinz Kling commanded the 13th Company of SS-Panzer Regiment 1, until succeeding Martin Gross in command of the regiment's 2nd Battalion during December 1943. In recognition of the many successes of the Tigers, Kling was awarded the Knight's Cross on February 23, 1944.

LAH Chief of Staff, Rudolf Lehmann, was awarded the Knight's Cross on February 23, 1944. It recognized his vital role in coordinating the actions of the division's battlegroups during the heavy fighting that winter. In this photo, Lehmann wears the less common cloth version of the German Cross in Gold. It was designed for the crews of vehicles, planes and submarines, for whom the metal version was unwieldy in close confines.

Wisch proposed SS-Panzergrenadier Regiment 2 commander Hugo Kraas for the Oak Leaves for his leadership at Kursk and in the late 1943 Ukrainian fighting. The award was approved on January 24, 1944, at which point he was ill and recovering from wounds. Kraas was able to obtain a set of Oak Leaves and posed in his dress tunic with his mother and five brothers. Boris Kraas, on the left, won the Knight's Cross posthumously on February 28, 1945, as the commander of SS-Panzerjäger Battalion 3. Helmut-Albrecht Kraas stands next to Boris, while German Army German Cross in Gold winner Emil Kraas is on the right.

Heinz Lammerding first commanded the Das Reich battlegroup that remained in Ukraine before taking command of the mass of the division that was rebuilding in France. He won the Knight's Cross on April 11, 1944 for his battlegroup leadership during heavy defensive fighting in February of that year. Below his Iron Cross First Class Lammerding wears the Commemorative Medal for the 1931 SA Rally in Brunswick. On his left sleeve is the Demyansk Shield, awarded for his service with Totenkopf in that campaign.

When Lammerding left the front, Otto Weidinger succeeded him in command of the much-reduced Das Reich battlegroup. Weidinger was awarded the Knight's Cross on April 21, 1944, officially for his command of Das Reich's Reconnaissance Battalion in heavy defensive fighting during November 1943. The recommendation for the award was written by Lammerding, and was considered to also represent Weidinger's leadership of the battlegroup. His decorations in this photo include Bronze grades of the Infantry Assault Badge and Close Combat Clasp, and the Wound Badge in Silver.

Alfred Lex grew up in the same small Austrian town as Sylvester Stadler, and likewise served in Regiment Der Führer. Lex was awarded the Knight's Cross on December 10, 1943 as the acting commander of his regiment's 2nd Battalion. When Weidinger took command of the Das Reich battlegroup, Lex became commander of the unit's remaining infantry elements. He was killed leading them on March 11, 1944, with his death notice indicating Lex held the Close Combat Clasp in Gold. This decoration is not listed in his file, but he appears to be wearing it in this photo, along with his documented Wound Badge in Gold. The Silver grades of these usually appear shinier in wartime photos.

Otto Meyer, commander of SS-Panzer Regiment 9, was the first Knight's Cross recipient in the Hohenstaufen Division. He received the decoration from his division commander Willi Bittrich, who is behind him in gray in this photo, shortly after its June 4, 1944 approval. Meyer's regiment had knocked out numerous Soviet guns and armored vehicles during the attempted relief of Tarnopol.

Werner Meyer was the acting commander of Germania's 1st Company during the Cherkassy fighting. He joined his battalion commander, Hans Dorr, in capturing the town of Shanderovka, which was a prerequisite for the successful break-out a few days later. For this, Meyer won the Knight's Cross on May 5, 1944. This photo is probably from a few weeks earlier, with the Knight's Cross added in. Meyer also wears the Close Combat Clasp in Silver, but won the Gold grade on April 12. Combined with his German Cross in Gold and Wound Badge in Gold, it made Meyer one of the most highly-decorated men in the German military, aside from those who won higher grades of the Knight's Cross.

Willy Hein was one of the leading officers of SS-Panzer Regiment 5. He was often at the most critical sector, launching counterattacks to support Wiking's infantry. This brought him both the German Cross and Gold and entry in the Honor Roll of the German Army during late 1943. Hein won the Knight's Cross on May 4, 1944 for actions at Cherkassy. As acting commander of the 2nd Company of his regiment, he had defended Wiking's supply troops against an unexpected Soviet attack. The attack was repulsed, and Hein then routed the Soviet force while pursuing their retreat. Along with his Knight's Cross and German Cross, this photo shows Hein with the Honor Roll Clasp on the ribbon of his Iron Cross Second Class. Note that while he was usually referred to as "Willi", Hein has signed this photo with the spelling "Willy".

Wiking commander Herbert Otto Gille was awarded the Swords to his Knight's Cross on February 20, 1944 for his division's role in the Cherkassy break-out. He poses with them here. Two months later, on April 19, Gille won the Diamonds after flying into surrounded Kovel and organizing its successful defense.

Walter Schmidt, still commanding Westland's 2nd Battalion, won the Oak Leaves on May 14, 1944. He had led his greatly-weakened battalion in successful combat in the autumn of 1943, and then led its remnants, along with many stragglers from other units, out of the Cherkassy pocket during the break-out.

Hermann Priess took command of Totenkopf following the Kharkov fighting. In his new post, he won the Oak Leaves on September 9, 1943 and the Swords on May 24 the next year. Both awards were proposed by 8th Army commander Otto Wöhler, who was impressed by the results Priess achieved with his greatly-depleted division in constant defensive fighting.

Karl Nicolussi-Leck commanded the Panthers of the 8th Company of SS-Panzer Regiment 5 in their first action, in late March 1944. On March 31, they broke through the encircling forces and reinforced the Kovel garrison, until the city could be relieved five days later. "Nico" was awarded the Knight's Cross on April 15. His decorations include the Golden Honor Badge of the Hitler Youth, earned while organizing Nazi activity in the ethnic-German community in the Italian South Tyrol.

In turn, Priess recommended Karl Ullrich for the Oak Leaves, which were awarded on May 14, 1944. Ullrich had repeatedly fought in the front line while leading the 3rd Battalion of SS-Panzergrenadier Regiment 5 Totenkopf at Kharkov and Kursk, and then commanding SS-Panzergrenadier Regiment 6 Theodor Eicke in Ukraine in the fall 1943 and spring 1944 fighting.

Away from the main fronts, the Nord Division was fighting in Soviet Karelia, near various Finnish units. After the Finnish armistice during September 1944, Nord retreated into Norway before being committed on the Western Front in early 1945.

The Prinz Eugen Division disarmed Italian units following Italy's withdrawal from the Axis. It fought in a series of brutal anti-partisan operations until suffering heavy losses against Soviet and Bulgarian forces while covering the German retreat from the Balkans in the autumn of 1944.

The SS-Cavalry Division mixed anti-partisan and front-line actions into the spring of 1944. It then rebuilt and gave up elements for the creation of a sister division. This second cavalry division has been referred to as the Maria Theresia Division, however, wartime documents don't use this title. The two SS cavalry divisions went into action in Hungary in the autumn of 1944. Surrounded in Budapest, they defended the city from the end of 1944 until being destroyed during the February 1945 break-out.

The Polizei, in its new configuration as a Panzergrenadier Division, also was part of the fighting in Hungary. After combat near the Romanian border, it held defensive positions north of Budapest.

The 1st SS-Infantry Brigade fought in the central part of the Eastern Front during 1943. In early 1944, it was withdrawn and used as the cadre for the Horst Wessel Panzergrenadier Division. A battlegroup fought in Galicia during the summer of 1944 before the entire division fought in Hungary in late 1944, alongside the Polizei, and in Silesia during 1945.

The 2nd SS-Infantry Brigade became a Latvian unit during the spring of 1943. It served in the Volkhov sector until early 1944, when it retreated to near the Latvian border and expanded into the 19th Waffen-Grenadier Division.

Gottlieb Renz held acting command of Nord's reserve force, SS-Motorized Infantry Battalion 6, during the heavy fighting the division faced at the end of June 1944. For this, he won the Knight's Cross on August 12 of that year. Renz also earned the Wound Badge in Silver at this time, awarded on July 7.

Franz Schreiber won the Knight's Cross on December 26, 1944. It recognized his command of SS-Mountain Regiment 12 Michael Gaissmair during Nord's retreat to Norway that autumn.

The Prinz Eugen Division's founder, Artur Phleps, had a long career in the Austro-Hungarian and Romanian armies. As such, he possessed a vast collection of decorations. Visible in this photo, besides the Knight's Cross he won on July 4, 1943 as Prinz Eugen commander, are the Clasp to his First World War Iron Cross Second Class, the Croatian Order of the Iron Trefoil and the Romanian Order of the Crown.

Phleps insisted that Bernhard Dietsche also be awarded the Knight's Cross, since his 2nd Battalion of SS-Volunteer Mountain Regiment 14 had spearheaded the German success during Operation Black, which had earned Phleps his Knight's Cross. Dietsche's award was approved on July 17, 1943. Here Dietsche poses with Prinz Eugen cuff title and collar patch, with runes to show full SS membership. His decorations include the Wound Badge in Silver and Infantry Assault Badge in Bronze.

Heinrich Petersen won the Knight's Cross on November 13, 1943 as commander of SS-Volunteer Mountain Regiment 13. He had achieved decisive success in disarming Italian units on the Dalmatian coast following Italy leaving the Axis, and in defending the area of the harbor of Split against Partisan and Italian attacks. Petersen wears the Croatian Order of the Crown of King Zvonimir First Class with Oak Leaves next to his Knight's Cross, and the Order of the Iron Trefoil Second Class next to his Iron Cross First Class.

The man most associated with the SS cavalry formations was Hermann Fegelein. He had commanded the SS-Calvary Brigade, and later commanded the SS-Cavalry Division. In between, he led an improvised battlegroup on the Don Front during December 1942. For this, he won the Oak Leaves on December 21. Just visible in this portrait is Fegelein's Riding Badge, awarded for equestrian sporting activities.

On August 29, 1943, the 4th Squadron of SS-Cavalry Regiment 15 was nearly destroyed while defending against Soviet attacks south-west of Kharkov. The Soviets could be seen assembling more men in a cornfield in front of the squadron's position. In desperation, the 4th Squadron commander Johannes Göhler led his last forty men on a charge into the cornfield. This surprise attack routed the Soviet force, giving the Germans time to reinforce their front. Göhler was awarded the Knight's Cross nineteen days later on September 17.

During the night of November 25/26, 1942, the positions of the 2nd Luftwaffe Field Division were penetrated, south of Rhzev. On his own initiative, Gustav Lombard moved his SS-Cavalry Regiment 15 into position to contain the breakthrough. He used aggressive patrolling to simulate greater strength, and the Soviet assault was successfully contained. Lombard was awarded the Knight's Cross months later on March 10, 1943.

Hermann Fegelein's younger brother Waldemar served under him in many assignments. Waldemar Fegelein won the Knight's Cross on December 16, 1943 as the commander of SS-Cavalry Regiment 16. During the previous September, in circumstances similar to Göhler's, he had inspired the remnants of his regiment to hold on in desperate defensive fighting near the Donets River, and had then led them in a counterattack that ended the threat in their sector.

Hans Diergarten, Chief of Staff of the SS-Cavalry Division, won the Knight's Cross on January 16, 1944. He had repeatedly distinguished himself in dealing with crises by leading improvised elements of his units in defensive or offensive actions. This was both with Hermann Fegelein's late-1942 battlegroup, and then with the SS-Cavalry Division. While cavalrymen normally earned the General Assault Badge, Diergarten had started his career as an infantryman and thus wears the Infantry Assault Badge in Silver.

A late-1943 group photo of five SS cavalry officers, all of whom eventually won the Knight's Cross. From the left are Siegfried Korth (February 9, 1945, as commander of the 3rd Squadron of SS-Cavalry Regiment 18), Hans-Georg von Charpentier (December 29, 1942, Korth's predecessor as commander of the 3rd Squadron of SS-Cavalry Regiment 18, then commander of the regiment), Gustav Lombard, Johannes Göhler, and Anton Vandieken (December 26, 1944, as commander of the 6th Squadron of SS-Cavalry Regiment 52).

Joachim Rumohr also won the Knight's Cross on January 16, 1944. He commanded the artillery regiment of the SS-Cavalry Division, but soon took command of the entire division, which by then had received the honor title Florian Geyer. Rumohr was killed in action, or committed suicide, during the failed break-out from Budapest.

Rumohr's counterpart, August Zehender, commanded the 22.SS-Volunteer Cavalry Division and was also killed during the Budapest break-out. He had won the Knight's Cross on March 10, 1943 as commander of SS-Cavalry Regiment 16. Rumohr and Zehender were both awarded the Oak Leaves for their leadership in Budapest, and both received advanced promotion to general rank during the fighting.

Fewer than 200 SS cavalrymen succeeded in reaching German lines during the February 1945 Budapest break-out. The most notable was Italian Army veteran Hermann Maringgele, who had led numerous patrols and counterattacks in Budapest. During the fighting, he accumulated his eighty-fourth day of close combat, the highest-known total of any German soldier during the Second World War. As a result, after the break-out he was received personally by Adolf Hitler on February 21. On that day, Maringgele was awarded the Knight's Cross and Close Combat Clasp in Gold, and was promoted to junior officer rank.

Johann Scherg won the Knight's Cross on October 23, 1944 as the commander of the 1st Company of SS-Armored Reconnaissance Battalion 4. In this photo, he also wears his Wound Badge in Gold, Close Combat Clasp in Silver and Panzer Assault Badge in Bronze. Scherg's shoulder boards have a Gothic "A" for "Aufklärungs" (reconnaissance).

During the fighting in the Banat, from where much of the Polizei's manpower came, Scherg's company had been surrounded and cut off. He directed his men in holding their position long enough for other German units to retreat, and then led a successful break-out back to German lines. This photo of Scherg receiving his Knight's Cross from Polizei Division commander Fritz Schmedes was taken around the end of October 1944.

Werner Hörnicke wears his many decorations after his December 1, 1943 award of the Knight's Cross. These include the German Sports Badge, the Infantry Assault Badge in Bronze and the Wound Badge in Gold. Hörnicke had commanded the 1st Battalion of SS-Infantry Regiment 10 in the 1st SS-Infantry Brigade during the German withdrawal from Smolensk, covering the retreat of other units.

Twenty-six days later, Karl Rubatscher, adjutant of the 1st Battalion of SS-Infantry Regiment 8, was awarded the Knight's Cross. During the Smolensk withdrawal, he had taken emergency command of his battalion, leading them in a successful break-out from encirclement. Rubatscher has a German Army eagle on his cap instead of the normal SS one.

When the Soviet offensive to capture Budapest erupted in early December 1944, the attacks were held up in the sector of the 18th SS-Volunteer Panzergrenadier Division by the 88mm anti-aircraft guns of the 1st Battery of SS-Flak Battalion 18. Dr Hans Lipinski, the acting battery commander, was awarded the Knight's Cross on January 2, 1945. He was an ethnic German from Bucovina and a veteran of the Romanian Army.

The Waffen-SS maintained a complex of specialized training schools at Beneschau, outside Prague. When the late-summer 1944 Slovak Rising occurred, SS-Regiment Schill was formed at Beneschau for emergency service in Slovakia. Hans Kettgen commanded the regiment's 1st Battalion and won the Knight's Cross on February 14, 1945. He had led the capture of the rebel stronghold of Banska Bystrica the previous October.

The SS-Sturmbrigade Dirlewanger became notorious for its cruelty and brutality during anti-partisan operations in the Soviet Union. Its founder and commander, Dr. Oskar Dirlewanger, was awarded the Knight's Cross on September 30, 1944, for his unit's ruthless actions against the population of Warsaw during the Polish Home Army's uprising in that city. In this carefully-posed photo, he also has the Slovak War Victory Cross under his Knight's Cross. Below his cloth German Cross in Gold is the Spanish Cross Dirlewanger earned during his service with the Condor Legion.

Friedrich Jeckeln was another of the SS leaders known for directing harsh and genocidal operations against Jews, partisans and other civilians. His anti-partisan units had to fight conventional combat in rearguard actions against the Red Army after the destruction of Army Group Center. This earned him the Knight's Cross on August 27, 1944.

The 3rd (Germanic) SS-Panzerkorps was formed during 1943 as the successor to the former Germanic legions. It was intended to include Wiking and its new sister division, Nordland. The leaders of the Dutch collaboration wanted the Dutch volunteers, whose numbers exceeded the Scandinavians, to have their own unit. Since Wiking was kept at the front, Nordland was instead joined by the SS-Panzergrenadier Brigade Nederland. The latter was a sort of mini-division, which gradually expanded into a full division by the end of the war. The German Army's Walloon Infantry Battalion was taken into the Waffen-SS, becoming the Assault Brigade Wallonien, while the Flemish Legion became the Assault Brigade Langemarck. Both were later given divisional status, though as with Nederland, all were under-strength (as were most German divisions in 1945).

Wallonien joined Wiking in Ukraine during October 1943, and remained with it through the Cherkassy break-out. Langemarck joined the Battlegroup Das Reich in the first days of 1944, also in Ukraine, and had to conduct a similar break-out from encirclement at Jampol. Both Belgian units then spent the balance of 1944 rebuilding, but during July sent small battalions to the Estonian front.

Nordland and Nederland were in place west of Leningrad by the first days of 1944. During the second half of January, they covered the German withdrawal to the Narva River line. There they were joined by the Estonian 20th Waffen-Grenadier Division for successful defensive fighting through the spring. In the last week of July, German forces in the Narva area withdrew to the Tannenberg Line prepared defenses, 20 kilometers to the west. These were held successfully, forcing the Soviets to attempt to outflank the line to the south. The outflanking was successfully countered by a division-sized battlegroup formed from elements of Nordland, Nederland and the Estonian Division, led by Nederland commander Jürgen Wagner. The Langemarck Battalion helped hold the Tannenberg Line, while the Wallonien Battalion fought with Battlegroup Wagner.

German defeats to the south forced the evacuation of Estonia during September 1944. Nordland and Nederland retreated to defensive positions in the Latvian province of Kurland, where they held out from October 1944 through the end of the following January. The battalions from Langemarck and Wallonien were withdrawn when the Germans left Estonia. They rejoined their parent formations, which were supposed to become divisions, following an influx of Belgian collaborationist refugees arriving in Germany in the wake of the Allied liberation of Belgium.

The Latvian 15th and 19th Waffen-Grenadier Divisions fought on the Latvian border in the spring and summer of 1944. The 19th Division then fought in Kurland until the end of the war.

Nordland and Nederland were sent to Pomerania at the beginning of February 1945. They were joined by the combat-ready elements of Langemarck and Wallonien for the failed Solstice offensive. This was followed by a gradual retreat across Pomerania and then defensive action against the Soviet Berlin offensive. Langemarck, Wallonien, and half of Nederland surrendered to Allied forces in the first days of May. The other half of Nederland was destroyed in the Halbe Pocket, south-east of Berlin, along with the 35th SS-Police-Grenadier Division and the Dirlewanger formation (upgraded to the 36th Waffen-Grenadier Division). Nordland was destroyed in Berlin, along with single battalions from the Latvian 15th Waffen-Grenadier Division and the French 33rd Waffen-Grenadier Division.

Walter Seebach was born in the Netherlands to German parents, and was a German citizen rather than a Dutch volunteer. During the late-January 1944 retreat to the Luga River and then to the Narva River, he was the acting commander of the 5th Company of SS-Panzergrenadier Regiment Danmark. On January 31, Regiment Danmark protected the bridge across the Luga River at Jamburg, when its lines were penetrated. If the bridge was lost, the retreat route for many German units would have been severed. Seebach, wounded in previous defensive fighting, led his company in a counterattack that made the continued retreat possible. This brought him the Knight's Cross on March 12, 1944. In this photo, Seebach also wears the Close Combat Clasp in Gold he was awarded four days later.

Nederland and Danmark held a bridgehead on the east bank of the Narva River, across from the town of Narva. A dozen or more Soviet tanks broke through Nederland's positions on March 14, 1944, almost reaching one of the bridges across the river. Philipp Wild, from the 1st Company of Nordland's SS-Panzer Battalion 11 Hermann von Salza, commanded one of the few available Panther tanks. With it, he intercepted the Soviet force, knocking out most of the enemy tanks. Wild was awarded the Knight's Cross on March 21, and poses here soon after with Rudolf Rott, his company commander. Rott was posthumously awarded the Knight's Cross on February 28, 1945 for his leadership during the Fourth Battle of Kurland.

The Soviets held small bridgeheads on the west bank of the Narva River, north of Narva. These were eliminated in fierce fighting during February 1944. When attacks on the final Soviet defenses at Vepsküla broke down, Estonian NCO Harald Nugiseks rallied his men twice, with the third assault finally eliminating the position. Nugiseks was awarded the Knight's Cross on April 9, 1944.

The Soviets tried to disrupt the German retreat to the Tannenberg Line by striking from the south through Auwere. The successful defense of that area was led by Harald Riipalu, commander of Waffen-Grenadier Regiment 45. Riipalu was awarded the Knight's Cross on August 23, 1944 and received it a few days later along with other successful soldiers of the Narva sector. In this photo, Felix Steiner is placing the Knight's Cross around Riipalu's neck, while Karl-Heinz Ertel and Christian Steenolt-Schütt look on. As a candidate for full SS membership, Riipalu wears SS runes on his left breast pocket.

After the late-August 1944 awards ceremony, this group shot portrayed the personalities. On the left and fourth from the left are 20th Waffen-Grenadier Division commander Franz Augsberger (Knight's Cross March 8, 1945) and Nordland Division commander Joachim Ziegler (Knight's Cross September 5, 1944). Between them are Riipalu and SS-Panzer Battalion 11 Hermann von Salza commander Paul-Albert Kausch (Knight's Cross August 23, 1944). The 3rd (Germanic) SS-Panzer Corps commander Felix Steiner is in the middle, next to SS-Artillery Regiment 54 commander Wilhelm Schlüter (Knight's Cross August 23, 1944). The final two men are artillery commander for the Narva area Paul Kresin (just received the German Cross in Gold) and Karl-Heinz Ertel, the adjutant of Nederland's De Ruyter Regiment (Knight's Cross August 23, 1944).

The successful defense of the Tannenberg Line was made possible, in part, by the tank-killing exploits of Flemish volunteer Remy Schrijnen from the Langemarck Battalion. On July 29, 1944 he single-handedly manned his anti-tank gun, knocking out numerous Soviet tanks and slowing their advance until Kausch could lead his armor in a counterattack. Schrijnen was awarded the Knight's Cross on September 21, 1944. He was awarded the Wound Badge in Gold, seen in this photo, on the same day.

The most exposed part of the Tannenberg Line was 'the finger'. This was held by the 2nd Battalion of the De Ruyter Regiment under the acting command of Helmut Scholz. He had already won the Knight's Cross in the Narva bridgehead, and was awarded the Oak Leaves on September 21, 1944. This portrait shows that Scholz also held the Close Combat Clasp in Silver, though his file only records him holding the Bronze grade.

Léon Degrelle was forbidden to return to combat after winning the Knight's Cross following the Cherkassy campaign. However, he joined the Wallonien Battalion after it arrived in Estonia, and took a moment to pose with Jürgen Wagner, in whose battlegroup the battalion fought. On the right is Karl Schäfer, who was nominally Degrelle's aide. He also had the secret mission of reporting Degrelle's activities to Heinrich Himmler.

The messenger squad in Helmut Scholz's headquarters of the 2nd Battalion of De Ruyter was led by Stefan Strapatin, an ethnic German from the Romanian Banat. During the Tannenberg Line fighting, he and Scholz both knocked out Soviet tanks near the headquarters with Panzerfaust anti-tank launchers. Strapatin knocked out two more Soviet tanks on September 24, during the retreat from Estonia. This helped secure the battalion's vehicles, which otherwise might have been captured. For his tank-killing feats Strapatin was awarded the Knight's Cross on November 16, 1944. Along with the Wound Badge in Silver and Panzer Assault Badge in Bronze, he wears four Tank Destruction Badges on his right sleeve.

The anti-tank platoon of the Wallonien Battalion was commanded by Walloon volunteer Leon Gillis. His guns held up the Soviet advance on August 22, which gave Degrelle time to organize a successful defense. Gillis was awarded the Knight's Cross on September 30, 1944. His decorations include the Close Combat Clasp in Silver, and on his shoulder boards is a Gothic "P" for "Pak" (worn by the anti-tank gun branch of service).

Fritz Knöchlein, notorious for the shooting of British PoWs at Le Paradis in 1940, made a successful career in Totenkopf and then its sister division Reichsführer-SS. In the spring of 1944, he took command of Norge, leading it through the Second Battle of Kurland in the autumn of that year. Knöchlein's energetic leadership of Norge in Kurland brought him the Knight's Cross on November 16, 1944. To show solidarity with his men, he wears his regiment's Norwegian arm flag and sunwheel collar patch.

Nikolajs Galdiņš was the most-highly decorated Latvian volunteer in the Waffen-SS. He was awarded the Knight's Cross on January 25, 1945 as the commander of Waffen-Grenadier Regiment 42 Voldemārs Veiss (named for the fallen first Latvian Knight's Cross winner). The Latvians successfully withstood the main effort of the Soviet offensive during the Third Battle of Kurland. Galdiņš' collar patch is the 'Fire Cross' (a traditional Latvian symbol) worn by the 19th Waffen-Grenadier Division, while below his German Cross in Gold is the medal for commemoration of a decade of Latvian independence.

Alfrēds Riekstiņš commanded a squad in Waffen-Fusilier Battalion 19. On March 17, 1945, during the Sixth Battle of Kurland, he led his men behind Soviet lines. They captured some heavy weapons and turned them on the Soviets, disrupting the Red Army forces enough for the front line to be restored. Almost three weeks later, on April 5, Riekstiņš was awarded the Knight's Cross. This is an actual Knight's Cross photo, as he was able to save the photo by escaping to Sweden at the end of the war. Sadly, Riekstiņš had to commit suicide after returning to Latvia as a British agent and being betrayed to the NKVD.

Danish Army officer Johannes Hellmers became the most highly-decorated Danish volunteer when he was awarded the Knight's Cross on March 5, 1945. Hellmers commanded the 6th Company of De Ruyter and led the remnants of his company in a decisive counterattack during the Fourth Battle of Kurland. His Totenkopf collar patch is from earlier service with Regiment Thule, and this photo is possibly a 1943 photo, modified to show his later awards of the German Cross in Gold and Knight's Cross.

The Germans knew that Allied forces would cross the English Channel and land in occupied Western Europe during the late spring or early summer of 1944. Since the intended landing spot wasn't known, the Germans were forced to disperse their armored units near coastal areas of France and Belgium. LAH was in Flanders on D-Day, June 6, and not ready for combat. Hitlerjugend had redeployed to eastern Normandy, which put it near to the invasion beaches. Das Reich was near Bordeaux, while Götz von Berlichingen (GvB) was in west-central France.

Hitlerjugend went into action on June 7, near Caen. It was soon forced into a defensive role, in which it was worn down over the following two months. GvB was next to arrive, fighting near Saint Lo, also in a defensive role. By the end of June, battlegroups from LAH and Das Reich were supporting the defensive efforts. Hohenstaufen and Frundsberg arrived in Normandy at about the same time. Instead of conducting a planned offensive into the area of the landing beaches, they were forced to conduct more localized counterattacks against the British advance in the Odon valley. Thereafter, they and the main bodies of LAH and Das Reich joined the other Waffen-SS divisions in holding defensive positions.

GvB was nearly destroyed by the time of the late-July Cobra offensive. Das Reich was badly mauled by Cobra, but still took part in the hopeless German offensive near Mortain, with the remnants of GvB attached. LAH also took part, while the other divisions continued defensive assignments. Much of Das Reich was outside of the eventual Falaise Pocket, and its energetic counterattacks cleared the way for the escape of many German units.

Hohenstaufen and Frundsberg fought their most famous battle during September 1944, when their remnants had a leading role in defeating the Market Garden offensive near Arnhem and Nijmegen. Also in the autumn, GvB was part of the Battle of Metz.

LAH, Das Reich, Hohenstaufen and Hitlerjugend (grouped as the 6th Panzer Army) all took part in the Ardennes Offensive, the Battle of the Bulge that began on December 16, 1944. After limited success, the offensive was contained. LAH and Hitlerjugend were rerouted from the northern sector to join the unsuccessful effort to take Bastogne. At the same time Frundsberg and GvB were part of the Nordwind Offensive in Alsace.

GvB remained on the Western Front for the rest of the war. The other divisions were sent east during January and February 1945. Frundsberg was committed in Pomerania for the Solstice Offensive, along with Polizei, while the 6th Panzer Army was sent to Hungary for the Spring Awakening Offensive. Prior to that operation, LAH and Hitlerjugend were used in the Southwind Offensive, which succeeded in destroying the Soviet Bridgehead across the Gran River. This success alerted the Soviets to the presence of the 6th Panzer Army in Hungary and the following Spring Awakening made little progress.

Wiking and Totenkopf had been refitted during the early summer of 1944. From mid-July, they helped contain the Soviet advance that followed the destruction of Army Group Center. They then held the "wet triangle" near Modlin, north of Warsaw, until the end of the year. Sent to Hungary at the start of 1945, the two divisions were part of three Konrad Offensives that attempted to restore the Margarethe Line defenses along the Danube and around Budapest. Once these failed, Totenkopf and Wiking took on a secondary role, holding defensive positions during Spring Awakening.

All the SS divisions in Hungary then retreated into Austria. After a failed effort to hold Vienna, they eventually made their made west to American captivity. Totenkopf was turned over to the Soviets, and stragglers from the others also went into Soviet captivity. The last official awards of the Knight's Cross were made on April 17, 1945. Unofficial awards continued after that date, due to Sepp Dietrich claiming he had been authorized to approve recommendations or because of the belief that the Dönitz government was approving all last-minute recommendations. Some of these awards were recognized after the war by the Association of Knight's Cross Bearers, as were some that survivors claim that Hitler made directly in Berlin on April 28 and 29.

Hans Weiss took command of SS-Heavy Tank Battalion 102 during the spring of 1944. At about that time, he is seen on the right with Alois Kalls, his 1st Company commander. Kalls won the Knight's Cross on August 23, 1944 for his company's success around Hill 112 during the second week of July. In this photo, Kalls wears the Wound Badge in Gold next to his Iron Cross First Class.

Cristian Tychsen salutes during a May 1944 parade in the southern French town of Caussade. By this time, he commanded SS-Panzer Regiment 2. Behind Tychsen is Dieter Kesten, his 2nd Battalion commander. Kesten had won the Knight's Cross on November 12, 1943 while commanding the regiment's 6th Company (whose ranks included Johan Thaler). This recognized his achievement on August 24 of that year during the final withdrawal from Kharkov. With only nine Panzer IVs available, Kesten and his men knocked out twenty-nine of sixty attacking Soviet tanks.

Das Reich had been heavily engaged in destroying Soviet bridgeheads on the west bank of the Dnieper River during October 1943. The 3rd Battery of SS-Assault Gun Battalion 2 played a leading role, since most of SS-Panzer Regiment 2 was in the rear area refitting. The battery's commander, Dr Wolfgang Roehder, led his guns from the front, ensuring their success. He had already distinguished himself during the summer and early autumn fighting, all of it contributing to his December 1, 1943 award of the Knight's Cross. This spring 1944 photo shows him after transferring to command of his battalion's 1st Battery, with 2nd Battery commander Hartmut Braun next to him.

Also during the Dnieper bridgehead fighting, on October 21 the firing position of the 1st Battalion of SS-Armored Artillery Regiment 2 was almost overrun. The acting commander of the battalion, Wolfgang Gast, rallied his gunners to fire on Soviet tanks at almost point-blank range. His battalion's defense prevented the linking up of two bridgeheads so that they could later be eliminated. Gast was awarded the Knight's Cross for this on June 4, 1944.

In another photo from the rebuilding of Das Reich in southern France, SS-Assault Gun Battalion 2 commander Ernst-August Krag is in the middle, with his battalion's surgeon Dr Georg Christian. At this point, Krag still wears the Wound Badge in Silver and Infantry Assault Badge in Bronze. On the left is Helmut Schreiber, now commanding the Deutschland Regiment's 3rd Battalion. He won the Close Combat Clasp in Gold on May 24, 1944 and appears to be wearing it in this photo.

Helmut Kämpfe was one of the most widely-decorated men in the Waffen-SS. By the time of this early 1944 photo, he was commander of Das Reich's armored half-track battalion, the 3rd Battalion of Regiment Der Führer. Kämpfe held the Knight's Cross (awarded December 10, 1943), the German Cross in Gold, the Wound Badge in Gold, the Close Combat Clasp in Gold and the General Assault Badge. On June 9, 1944 he was captured by the French Resistance and killed the next day. The search for Kämpfe resulted in the mass killing of civilians at Oradour-sur-Glane on June 10.

Heinz Macher, still in command of Deutschland's 16th (Combat Engineer) Company, poses in early 1944 with platoon commander Ewald Ehm, left, and squad leader Kurt "Jonny" Förster. A variety of insignia can be seen, the most unusual being Ehm's sleeve badge for being a qualified coxswain for Engineer Assault Boats.

Sepp Dietrich, as commander of the 1st SS-Panzer Corps, inspects SS-Panzergrenadier Regiment 1 in the late spring of 1944. By this time, he wore the Swords to his Knight's Cross with Oak Leaves. Behind him are the regiment's commander, Albert Frey, and LAH commander Teddy Wisch, both wearing the Oak Leaves.

On June 13, 1944 the German defenses around Caen were outflanked by a British advance through Villers-Bocage. The crisis was averted by a counterattack involving elements of the Panzer Lehr Division and the 2nd Company of SS Heavy Tank Battalion 101, the latter commanded by Michael Wittmann. For this action, Wittmann was awarded the Swords to his Knight's Cross with Oak Leaves on June 22. He is seen wearing them in this, a still from a German newsreel.

Another newsreel still shows Sepp Dietrich with officers of Hitlerjugend. Max Wünsche and Kurt Meyer stand in the rear, while Dietrich is flanked by Wilhelm Mohnke and Karlheinz Prinz, who have just been presented with their Knight's Crosses. Mohnke's award was approved on July 11, 1944 for his command of SS-Panzergrenadier Regiment 26 in the defense of Caen. Prinz's was approved the same day for his command of the 2nd Battalion of SS-Panzer Regiment 12 in the preceding weeks.

Hans Waldmüller was awarded the Knight's Cross on August 27, 1944 as the commander of the 1st Battalion of SS-Panzergrenadier Regiment 25. He had distinguished himself throughout the Normandy campaign, and his battalion played a major role in slowing the Canadian advance on Falaise. Waldmüller was killed by Belgian partisans twelve days after his Knight's Cross was approved, and this photo probably shows the decoration added in.

Sepp Dietrich was awarded the Diamonds to his Knight's Cross with Oak Leaves and Swords on August 8, 1944. This photo is from two days later, when he visited Hitler's headquarters to receive the decoration. Dietrich's collar insignia reflects his August 1 promotion to SS-Oberst-Gruppenführer. He and Paul Hausser were the only Waffen-SS officers to achieve that rank.

During the fighting near St Lo, following D-Day, Regiment Deutschland was credited with repulsing sixty-three American attacks, fifty-six of them supported by armor. The regimental reserve, formed from the combat engineers of the 16th Company and the motorcycle platoon of the regimental Staff Company, launched thirty-eight counterattacks during this time. The 16th Company's commander, Heinz Macher, was awarded the Oak Leaves on August 19, 1944. He had earned the Wound Badge in Gold and Close Combat Clasp in Silver in the months since his Knight's Cross award. Macher later earned the Close Combat Clasp in Gold, but appears to be wearing the Silver grade in this photo.

The motorcycle platoon commander, Adolf Rüd, was awarded the Knight's Cross on August 23, 1944, twenty-one days after he had been killed in action. This photo has had the Knight's Cross and part of his rank insignia added in. While Macher had the older Gothic script regimental cuff-title, Rüd wore the later Latin script version.

Also on August 23, 1944, Kämpfe's successor Heinz Werner was awarded the Knight's Cross as the acting commander of the 3rd Battalion of Regiment Der Führer. During the first weeks of July, 1944, Werner and his battalion had supported the badly-depleted 353rd Infantry Division, helping make their successful defense possible.

One more Das Reich Knight's Cross award winner on August 23, 1944 was Adolf Reeb, a platoon commander in the 7th Company of SS-Panzer Regiment 2. Just as Werner's battalion had supported the 353rd Infantry Division, the 7th Company and its parent 2nd Battalion had supported the also-depleted GvB Division during the first half of July. For this, Reeb was awarded the Knight's Cross and his company commander, Karl Kloskowski, received the Oak Leaves.

Hans Schabschneider was the ammunition supply NCO for the 4th Battery of SS-Armored Artillery Regiment 2. When Das Reich was caught in the Roncey Pocket, he collected thirty stragglers and led them in the capture of an American supply column. Schabschneider returned to German lines with 12 captured trucks and roughly 100 prisoners. He was awarded the Knight's Cross on August 27, 1944.

Adolf Peichl was well-known in Regiment Der Führer for his tank-killing exploits. He finished the war with eleven confirmed enemy tanks destroyed, and was one of the first to be awarded the Close Combat Clasp in Gold, which he wears here along with his Wound Badge in Gold. As part of the staff of the 12th Company of his regiment, Peichl led a counterattack on September 13, 1944 that recaptured some Westwall bunkers that had been occupied by American forces. This brought him the Knight's Cross a month later on October 16.

The 1st Battery of SS-Armored Anti-Tank Battalion 12 saw its first action in the defense of the Canadian advance on Falaise during the second week of August 1944. Rudolf Roy commanded a platoon in the battery, and for its success was awarded the Knight's Cross on October 16, 1944.

Roy actually received his Knight's Cross in a ceremony in late October. Also honored that day was his battery commander Georg Hurdelbrink and Arnold Jürgensen, the commander of the 1st Battalion of SS-Panzer Regiment 12. They had also won their award on October 16, 1944. Hurdelbrink's recognized the same actions for which Roy was decorated, while Jürgensen's was for the part his Panthers played in repeated counterattacks around Hill 112 and then north of Falaise. Jürgensen is shaking the hand of Hitlerjugend Division Chief of Staff Hubert Meyer.

Hitlerjugend was awarded three additional Knight's Crosses on November 18, 1944. One was to Fritz Eckstein, who served as gunner in Georg Hurdelbrink's command Jagdpanzer IV. The second was to Bernhard Krause, who was now commander of SS-Panzergrenadier Regiment 26, but had commanded his regiment's 1st Battalion during the fighting around Caen. This group photo shows, from the left: Eckstein, 6th Panzer Army Chief of Staff Fritz Kraemer, unknown, 6th Panzer Army commander Sepp Dietrich, another unknown, Krause, and newly-appointed Hitlerjugend Division commander Hugo Kraas.

The third Hitlerjugend member to be awarded the Knight's Cross on November 18 was Richard Rudolph. In Normandy, SS-Panzer Regiment 12 had included a temporary 9th Company. Rudolph had commanded a platoon in this company, and knocked out several British tanks during the Goodwood Offensive near Carpiquet airfield. His platoon's effort had aided the defense by Krause's men.

The remnants of Hohenstaufen that fought near Arnhem were led by the division's Chief of Staff, Walter Harzer. His success in defeating the British airborne landing was recognized through the immediate award of the Knight's Cross on September 21, 1944. Four days later, a formal recommendation was filed to provide official justification for the decoration.

Karl-Heinz Euling commanded a battalion in Hohenstaufen. Just before Market Garden, the battalion was transferred to Frundsberg, where it became the 1st Battalion of SS-Panzergrenadier Regiment 22. Euling and his battalion defended the Nijmegen bridge long enough to prevent advancing British armored units from linking up with the airborne forces at Arnhem and Oosterbeek. Euling was awarded the Knight's Cross on October 15 or 17, with both dates in his file. Though he excelled as a combat officer, Euling's past as an administrative officer is shown by the War Merit Cross First Class, with swords, worn under his Iron Cross First Class.

Ludwig Kepplinger's career progressed rapidly after his Knight's Cross award. By the spring of 1944, he took command of SS-Panzer Battalion 17 in GvB. On August 6 of that year, he was traveling behind the front line in his command car when it was ambushed by French Resistance fighters. Kepplinger died after being hit by six bullets.

Ortwin Kuske and Fred Papas from SS-Armored Reconnaissance Battalion 17, after Papas received his Knight's Cross in Alsace in early 1945.

Kuske was the acting commander of his battalion's 3rd Company during the November 1944 fighting around Metz. Kuske and his men held up an American attack that threatened the 416th Volksgrenadier Division. When their position could no longer be held, instead of surrendering, he led a successful break-out. Kuske was awarded the Knight's Cross on November 26, 1944. He appears to wear the Wound Badge in Gold, though this isn't indicated in his file.

Papas was the adjutant of his battalion when commander Kurt Wahl was wounded. With twenty men of the battalion headquarters, Papas fought off an attack by two American battalions, which saved GvB from being outflanked. Papas was awarded the Knight's Cross on December 27, 1944.

Kurt Wahl had won the Knight's Cross on August 23, 1944 as the adjutant of SS-Panzergrenadier Regiment 37. After taking command of SS-Armored Reconnaissance Battalion 17, he was awarded the Oak Leaves on February 1, 1945.

Franz Frauscher was a platoon commander in the 4th Company of SS-Panzer Regiment 2. He was awarded the Knight's Cross on December 31, 1944, a week after knocking out many American tanks while his regiment attempted to advance through Manhay in the Ardennes on Christmas Eve.

Der Führer Regiment commander Otto Weidinger was awarded the Oak Leaves the day after Christmas, 1944. The decoration actually recognized his leadership of the regiment in counterattacking into the Falaise Pocket to create an escape route for the encircled forces. This photo, after receiving the Oak Leaves, also displays Weidinger's Wound Badge in Silver and Bronze grade of the Close Combat Clasp and the Infantry Assault Badge.

Heinrich Schmelzer commanded the 1st Company of SS-Combat Engineer Battalion 2 in the Ardennes. On January 7 and 8, 1945 he guarded Das Reich's retreat after the unit on his flank was destroyed, allowing the division to avoid a crisis. For this, Schmelzer was awarded the Oak Leaves on February 28. This photo appears to have been taken after the award was announced but before it was presented. Schmelzer's Knight's Cross was hung lower than normal, giving room for the Oak Leaves to be added in for publication in newspapers.

No authentic Oak Leaves photo is known to have survived for Ernst-August Krag. His award was approved on the same day as Schmeltzer's. His SS-Armored Reconnaissance Battalion 2 had held out against much stronger American forces during the first week of January 1945, also contributing to Das Reich's successful withdrawal. This portrait shows Krag's later awards, including the Wound Badge in Gold and the Panzer Assault Badge for twenty-five engagements. His file indicates he won the Close Combat Clasp in Silver, but known photos only show him wearing the Bronze grade.

Josef Rölleke commanded the messenger squad in the headquarters of SS-Panzergrenadier Regiment 5 Totenkopf. On March 27, 1944, near Balta, he was ordered to lead five men on a reconnaissance patrol to check Soviet strength around a bridge his battalion would need for an anticipated retreat. Exceeding his orders, Rölleke and his patrol actually captured the bridge intact. For this, he was awarded the Knight's Cross on June 16, 1944. Rölleke's decorations in this portrait show a great contrast between his Silver Close Combat Clasp and Wound Badge and Bronze Panzer Assault Badge.

Sudeten German Johann Fiedler was also awarded the Knight's Cross on June 16, 1944 as a platoon leader in the 4th Company of SS-Panzergrenadier Regiment 6 Theodor Eicke. When his regiment's attack on April 27, 1944 had bogged down, Fiedler on his own initiative led his platoon in clearing an area of Soviet defenses. He had already won the Wound Badge in Gold, which he wears here, along with the Demyansk Shield at his left shoulder. This was presented to German Army and Waffen-SS survivors of the 1942 fighting in the Demyansk Fortress.

Another Sudeten Knight's Cross winner was Egon Franz, an acting platoon commander in the 3rd Company of SS-Panzergrenadier Regiment 9 Germania. During the first of three defensive battles north of Warsaw on August 25, 1944, this company launched decisive counterattacks on Soviet forces that had penetrated German Army positions. Franz likely was decorated for his role in these actions, as his Knight's Cross was approved on October 16, 1944.

Hermann Lang's file is incomplete. He won the Knight's Cross on October 23, 1944 as the leader of the messenger staff in the headquarters of the 1st Battalion of Regiment Totenkopf, following costly defensive fighting north of Warsaw. In this portrait, Lang wears the Wound Badge in Silver and Close Combat Clasp in Silver, neither of which he was recorded as possessing.

During the third defensive battle north of Warsaw, Eberhard Heder, commander of SS-Armored Combat Engineer Battalion 5, was assigned to lead an improvised emergency force formed from Wiking's supply troops. For three days starting on October 13, he led these men in plugging a gap in the front line. Even though eventually surrounded, Heder and his men repulsed twenty-one attacks and launched numerous counterattacks until a relief force could be assembled. Heder was awarded the Knight's Cross on November 18, 1944.

Otto Skorzeny, the commander of the SS Raiding Detachments, commanded the German units in a bridgehead at Schwedt on the east side of the Oder River during the spring of 1945. This photo shows him at Schwedt, as there is no known photo of Skorzeny with the Oak Leaves he was awarded on April 9, 1945.

This photo of SS-Panzer Regiment 1 commander Joachim Peiper and SS-Panzer Regiment 12 commander Martin Gross is usually said to have been taken in Austria during the last weeks of the war. In fact, it was taken near the Hungarian town of Parkany (today part of Slovakia and known as Štúrovo) on February 19, 1945 during the South Wind Offensive that destroyed the Soviet bridgehead on the west bank of the Gran River.

Das Reich endured heavy fighting in Vienna during early April 1945. While most photos from the last weeks of the war were destroyed or captured, a sequence featuring Der Führer Regiment commander Otto Weidinger in Vienna survived. This is one of them, showing Weidinger taking a cigarette break with his 3rd (Armored Half-Track) Battalion commander Heinz Werner. On May 6, 1945, Weidinger was awarded the Swords and Werner was awarded the Oak Leaves. These were both "Dietrich awards" that are considered unofficial but were accepted by the Organization of Knight's Cross Bearers.

Though born in Switzerland, Emil Seibold was a German citizen. Between the spring of 1943 and the end of the war, he was credited with sixty-nine enemy tanks destroyed, while only commanding Panzer IVs and captured T34s. This photo was taken to commemorate his 1944 award of the German Cross in Gold, but has later had the Knight's Cross added in. Seibold was another of the May 6, 1945 "Dietrich award" Knight's Cross winners for his service as a platoon commander in the 8th Company of SS-Panzer Regiment 2.

Gustav-Peter Reber was a company commander in the headquarters of the 11th SS-Panzerkorps. He was awarded the Knight's Cross on April 28, 1945 during the retreat from the Oder River and the Halbe Pocket. Reber's award was supposed to originate from Hitler's headquarters, though relevant records have been lost. However, Reber's award was accepted by the Organization of Knight's Cross Bearers. His decorations in this earlier photo include the Wound Badge in Gold.

Further Reading

A vast literature exists about the history of the Waffen-SS, in numerous languages. Those interested specifically in the winners of the Knight's Cross will learn more about these men, and the context in which they won their decorations, in the following English-language works. They form a starting point, but the list is not exhaustive, and is heavily based on books by veterans, or written with their assistance. This has the natural tendency of placing the award winners in the best possible light. The Finnish academic study included below is easily available online at the time of writing, and provides useful balance, since it includes information on several Waffen-SS Knight's Cross winners.

Angolia, John R. *For Führer and Fatherland: Military Awards of the Third Reich*. San Jose, Bender, 1987.

Berger, Florian. *The Face of Courage: The 98 Men Who Received Both the Knight's Cross and the Close Combat Clasp in Gold*. Winnipeg, Fedorowicz, 2007.

Husemann, Friedrich. *In Good Faith: The History of the 4th SS-Polizei-Panzergrenadier Division volumes 1–2*. Winnipeg, Fedorowicz, 2003–2009.

Klapdor, Ewald. *Viking Panzers: The German 5th SS Tank Regiment in the East in World War II*. Mechanicsburg, PA, Stackpole, 2011.

Lehmann, Rudolf and Ralf Tiemann. *The Leibstandarte volumes I–IV/2*. Winnipeg, Fedorowicz, 1987–2008.

Meyer, Hubert. *Hitlerjugend: The History of the 12. SS-Panzer Division*. Winnipeg, Fedorowicz, 1994.

Miller, Michael D. *Knight's Cross Holders of the SS and German Police volume 1*. Solihull, UK, Helion, 2016.

Schneider, Jost W. *Their Honor Was Loyalty!, An Illustrated and Documentary History of the Knight's Cross Holders of the Waffen-SS and Police 1940-1945*. San Jose, Bender, 1993.

Tieke, Wilhelm. *Horst Wessel: The Combat History of the 18th SS-Panzergrenadier Division*. Winnipeg, Fedorowicz, 2015.

Ullrich, Karl. *Like a Cliff in the Ocean: The History of the 3. SS-Panzer-Division "Totenkopf."* Winnipeg, Fedorowicz, 2002.

Weidinger, Otto. *Das Reich volumes I–V*. Winnipeg, Fedorowicz, 1990–2012.

Westerlund, Lars. *The Finnish SS-Volunteers and Atrocities Against Jews, Civilians and Prisoners of War in Ukraine and the Caucasus Region 1941–1943*. Helsinki, The National Archives of Finland, 2019.

Yerger, Mark C. *German Cross in Gold Holders of the SS and Police volumes 1–8*. San Jose, Bender, 2003–2015.

Yerger, Mark C., and Ignacio Arrondo. *Totenkopf volumes 1–2*. Solihull, UK, Helion, 2015–2016.